Lace YARN STUDIO

Lace YARN STUDIO

GARMENTS, HATS, AND
FRESH IDEAS FOR LACE YARN

Carol J. Sulcoski

LARK

New York

An Imprint of Sterling Publishing
1166 Avenue of the Americas
New York, NY 10036

ISBN 978-1-4547-0861-2

Distributed in Canada by Sterling Publishing
c/o Canadian Manda Group, 664 Annette Street
Toronto, Ontario, Canada M6S 2C8
Distributed in the United Kingdom by GMC Distribution Services
Castle Place, 166 High Street, Lewes, East Sussex, England BN7 1XU
Distributed in Australia by Capricorn Link (Australia) Pty. Ltd.
P.O. Box 704, Windsor, NSW 2756, Australia

For information about custom editions, special sales, and premium and
corporate purchases, please contact Sterling Special Sales at 800-805-5489
or specialsales@sterlingpublishing.com.

Manufactured in China

2 4 6 8 10 9 7 5 3 1

larkcrafts.com

Contents

preface

WHEN YOU HEAR THE PHRASE "lace weight yarn," what do you see? Heirloom shawls in intricate patterns, so airy they can slide through a wedding ring? Floral motifs in pastel colors, with tons of ruffles and frills? Complex pattern stitches with names like "lily of the valley" and "peacock's tail" or tiny nupps painstakingly worked in Shetland wool?

Projects knit in lace weight yarn can be all of those things—but they don't have to be. Lace weight projects can be dramatic instead of frilly, knit in deep colors and unexpected fibers instead of pastel-colored wool. Instead of floral motifs, lace weight projects can showcase geometric patterns or strikingly simple rows of eyelets. Shawls and stoles are wonderful pieces to knit in superfine yarns, but so are gloves, tanks, and pullovers. Just because you're not the flowery shawl type doesn't mean there aren't plenty of lace weight projects for you.

When you envision yourself knitting something in lace weight yarn, what do you imagine? Struggling with yarn that makes dental floss look chunky? Marking off row upon row of charts, with the occasional interruption to rip out mistakes? Complex stitch patterns without a single plain row to relax in? Projects that will be breathtaking when finished, but are so all-consuming that they take months or years to complete?

Lace weight knitting often involves charts and complex patterning, and may take a long time to finish—but it doesn't have to. Jacking up the gauge or using multiple strands of yarn together can make projects zip by while creating unique and striking effects. Lace weight

knitting traditionally is done using "lace" patterns—skillfully arranged increases and decreases that form decorative motifs—but it can just as easily be done using slip stitches, cables, or humbler patterns like Stockinette and Garter stitch. Knitting an exquisitely complex shawl is fun (at least for some knitters!) but if you're like me, less elaborate items will get finished faster, and layering pieces will be more useful in your day-to-day wardrobe.

My previous book, *Sock Yarn Studio*, celebrated the joys of sock yarn for items other than socks. In this book, I'll present a collection of patterns that use lace weight yarn for things other than traditional lace shawl knitting. I know there are knitters out there who have gorgeous lace weight yarns in their stash but aren't quite sure what to do with them. I have seen knitters fondle luscious skeins of bison or silk in a yarn shop, then hesitate to bring them home for fear they have no time for elaborate chart-following. I know there are knitters, like me, who appreciate the beauty of lace shawls, but find wearing them on a daily basis to be impractical. (The third or fourth time your lace shawl ends up dunked in your coffee, you reconsider wearing it . . .)

This book, my friends, is for you. My aim is to bust open the stereotypes about lace weight yarn. I'll show you wonderful things you can make from lace weight yarn including pullovers, a hat, a pillow cover and even a necklace. I'll show you tricks, like plying strands of lace weight together, or working in expanded gauges, to help speed your lace-yarn knitting along. My talented designer friends will inspire you with their use of techniques not traditionally associated with superfine yarns (cables? slip stitches?) and when you're ready to settle back with some easier projects, we'll include some of those, too. If you're new to lace weight yarn, don't fret: this book includes plenty of technical information to get you started, along with tips and tricks for making your lace yarn knitting fun.

Disclaimers
(or once a lawyer, always a lawyer)

Before we get into the real knitting stuff, let's talk about what is and isn't in this book. This book is devoted to the joys of lace weight yarn—but for knitting items other than those typically found in most "laceknitting" books. There are many beautiful books devoted to traditional lace knitting and I've included one or two of my favorites in the Appendix in case you decide to explore that wonderful world later. But please don't send me cranky emails asking me how I could write a book about lace weight yarns without including a single Estonian nupp! That's just not what this book is about.

This book is designed for someone who already knows the basics of knitting. If you don't yet know how to knit, then this book isn't going to teach you. If you are a relatively new knitter, though, don't worry; the patterns in this book span all difficulty levels. Many of the projects in this book can easily be done by less-experienced knitters; other projects may stretch your skills a little but to help your comfort level, we've used inset boxes to help walk you through any unusual or advanced techniques.

This book focuses on a category of yarns traditionally called "lace weight," and identified as "Superfine—Category 0" on the Craft Yarn Council's Standard Yarn Weight System. We'll talk about this in more detail later, but suffice it to say that the patterns in this book are designed to work with lace weight yarn, rather than heavier weights of yarn. Be advised that using a different category of yarn will result in a finished item that is larger and heavier, perhaps substantially so, than the finished dimensions listed in the pattern. Even if you're able to get a similar gauge from a thicker yarn, your finished project might not have the airy look or drape of a garment knit in true lace weight yarn.

ALL ABOUT *Lace* WEIGHT YARN

I'm sure you're eager to begin the beautiful knitting projects, but before we cast on a single stitch, we need to talk a little bit about lace weight yarn—in particular, what it is and how to use it.

it's superfine

I TEACH A LOT OF CLASSES that delve into the mysteries of yarn classification, and as my starting point, I use the Craft Yarn Council's Standard Yarn Weight system.

At its most basic, this chart places various yarns into categories, from thinnest to thickest. Each category is assigned a number and a name, and each category has a typical gauge and needle size that tend to work best with yarns of that category. When you take a look at the CYC chart, you can find lace weight yarn in the far left-hand column, labeled Category 0 – Lace.[1]

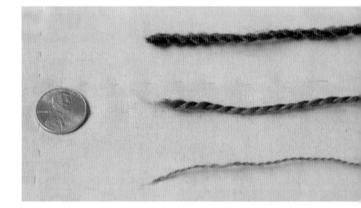

Because of the way that the CYC chart is organized you can immediately see that lace weight yarn is the finest, thinnest category of yarn typically used for knitting. You can see by looking at a strand of Category 0 yarn how thin and fine it is.

Even a skein of lace weight yarn that contains 900 or more yards still feels light as a feather when you pick it up. It's the fineness of a lace weight yarn that makes it both intoxicating and intimidating.

[1]Why does the chart begin with Category 0 and not Category 1? When this chart was first adopted, there was no separate category for superfine yarns. Lace weight yarns were lumped together with fingering weight yarns (including sock yarn). Eventually, the creators of the chart realized that lace weight yarns needed their own category. Since the smallest existing category was called "Category 1," they had to name the new category "Category 0."

Standard Yarn Weight System

Categories of yarn, gauge ranges, and recommended needle and hook sizes

Yarn Weight Symbol and Category Names	**0** LACE	**1** SUPER FINE	**2** FINE	**3** LIGHT	**4** MEDIUM	**5** BULKY	**6** SUPER BULKY
Type of yarns in category	Fingering 10-count crochet thread	Sock, Fingering, Baby	Sport, Baby	DK, Light Worsted	Worsted, Afghan, Aran	Chunky, Craft, Rug	Bulky, Roving
Knit Gauge Range* in Stockinette Stitch to 4 inches	33–40** sts	27–32 sts	23–26 sts	21–24 st	16–20 sts	12–15 sts	6–11 sts
Recommended Needle in Metric Size Range 1.5–2.25	mm 2.25–3.25	mm 3.25–3.75	mm 3.75–4.5	mm 4.5–5.5	mm 5.5–8	mm 8 mm	and larger
Recommended Needle U.S. Size Range	000–1	1 to 3	3 to 5	5 to 7	7 to 9	9 to 11	11 and larger
Crochet Gauge* Ranges in Single Crochet to 4 inch	32–42 double crochets**	21–32 sts	16–20 sts	12–17 sts	11–14 sts	8–11 sts	5–9 sts
Recommended Hook in Metric Size Range	Steel*** 1.6–1.4 mm	2.25–3.5 mm	3.5–4.5 mm	4.5–5.5 mm	5.5–6.5 mm	6.5–9 mm	9 mm and larger
Recommended Hook U.S. Size Range	Steel*** 6, 7, 8 Regular hook B–1	B–1 to E–4	E–4 to 7	7 to I–9	I–9 to K–10½	K–10½ to M–13	M–13 and larger

* GUIDELINES ONLY: The above reflect the most commonly used gauges and needle or hook sizes for specific yarn categories.

** Lace weight yarns are usually knitted or crocheted on larger needles and hooks to create lacy, openwork patterns. Accordingly, a gauge range is difficult to determine. Always follow the gauge stated in your pattern.

*** Steel crochet hooks are sized differently from regular hooks—the higher the number, the smaller the hook, which is the reverse of regular hook sizing.

needles & gauge

KNITTERS WHO ARE USED TO WORKING WITH thicker yarns know that, generally speaking, when you move from one category of yarn to the next, your gauge and needle size will change too. And even those who claim not to know much about yarn weight intuitively know that you tend to knit bigger yarn on bigger needles and skinny yarn on smaller needles. (Check out the suggested needle sizes for each category on the CYC chart and you'll see what I mean). Smaller needles make smaller stitches, while bigger needles make bigger stitches. Generally speaking, you can fit more stitches per inch using a fine yarn than you can using a thicker yarn, and once again, the CYC chart's suggested gauge row shows this.

That means that when you go all the way down to the thinnest category of yarn, Category 0, you must be knitting on teeny-tiny needles (size 0 or smaller) at a gauge of 8 or more stitches per inch, right?

Not necessarily.

When discussing lace weight yarns with my students, I always warn them that even though a knitter could knit lace weight yarn on toothpick-sized needles, people rarely do. Instead, they play with stitch patterns and needle sizes that will give them airy, loosely-knit fabric, the kind with bigger holes between the stitches, rather than dense, tightly-knit fabric. To get airy fabric, you have to knit on needles that are proportionately larger than the yarn might otherwise require, needles that will create bigger-than-typical holes in the fabric. Consider these two swatches. Both are knit in the same lace weight yarn, but on very different needle sizes. The swatch on the top was knit using size 0 needles; the swatch on the bottom with size 6 needles. See the difference?

Because lace weight yarns are so often knit at larger-than-typical gauges, working with them does not mean you will necessarily be using microscopically thin needles—in fact, most of the time, you'll be knitting with the same sized needles you use on other, thicker weights of yarn.

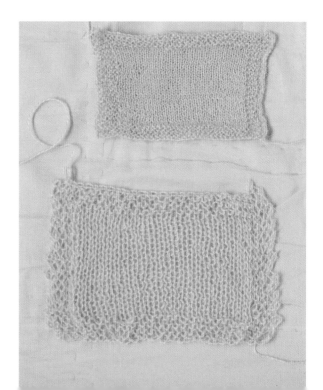

You'll see this reflected on the Craft Yarn Council's chart and on many lace weight yarn labels, where suggested needle size and gauge for the lace weight category are given as a broad range, spanning many needles sizes and stitches per inch.

Indeed, if you flip through the projects in this book, you'll see that the required gauge varies from 3½ stitches per inch, all the way up to 8 stitches per inch—a very wide range. And the vast majority of projects were knit at a gauge of 5 or fewer stitches per inch. Think about it: 5 stitches per inch is the same gauge you get when knitting worsted weight yarn. So much for assuming that all lace weight projects are super-slow to finish!

IF YOU'RE STILL NOT CONVINCED . . .

One of the reasons I wanted to write this book was because I think lace weight yarn gets a bad rap. I wasn't always a fan of fine-gauge yarns myself; I vividly remember having a conversation with a local yarn store clerk about yarns, wrinkling my nose up at anything thinner than worsted weight! I was wrong about fine yarns, and it wasn't until I started playing with them that I realized just how many advantages fine yarns, particularly lace weight yarns, have.

- They are lightweight. I am someone whose internal thermostat always runs to the warm side. Sweaters knit in bulky yarns make me, to put it

indelicately, sweat. I also happen to live in a geographic area that doesn't often get Arctic-chilly weather. A light-as-air lace weight yarn makes a wrap or cardigan that I can wear in comfort most of the year, rather than only a handful of the coldest winter days.

- They come in a staggering variety. Lace weight yarns come in just about every type of fiber you can imagine (Merino? Blue-faced Leicester? Silk? Bamboo? Alpaca? Tencel?). Because lace weight yarns use a relatively small amount of fiber per yard, they also come in rare and exotic fibers that aren't often spun into thicker blends because the cost is prohibitive. How about American bison down? Yak? Fiber from the Canadian musk ox known as qiviut? New Zealand possum (which, trust me, is not at all like the "possum" we have where I live)? You'll find gorgeous blends that marry the best qualities of two or more fibers. You'll find commercially-dyed solid yarns; semi-solid handpaints; multicolored spacedyes and handpaints; self-striping; yarns with different colored plies; and more.

- They are versatile. Yes, you can knit gorgeous lace shawls with superfine yarn, but you can also knit spectacular layering pieces, warm-weather shells, light-as-air cowls, gauntlets, even skirts! Anything a thicker yarn can do a thin yarn can do, too.

- Their fine diameter makes them perfect for plying. Because lace weight yarns are so thin, you can

double- or even triple-strand them to create interesting effects. Longing for a blend of tencel plus mink? Strand two lace weights together and build the yarn of your dreams. Use yarns in the same palette and see the subtle textural interplay. Or mix yarns of different hues and create multicolored yarns that never pool.

✂ They are economical. Thinner yarns contain less fiber and therefore cost less than their thicker cousins. A sweater that takes 1000 yarns of lace weight yarn can cost as little as $30, whereas a sweater knit in bulky weight yarn might cost three to five times that much. That also means you can make projects from much higher-quality fibers for the same or less money than if you were making a comparable project in a thicker weight of yarn.

✂ Superfine yarns can do things thick yarns can't. Have you ever made a softly-flowing wrap from a chunky yarn, or tried to knit a rippling ruffled edge or soft ruching with a bulky yarn? A tank, a whisper-soft skirt, a semi-sheer sweater—all are tough or impractical to create with thick yarns.

IDENTIFYING TRUE LACE WEIGHT YARN

Now that I've convinced you why you need to be knitting with lace weight yarns, let's talk about how to find them. It's unfortunate but true: not everyone understands the ins and outs of yarn substitution, and even well-informed knitters don't always know how to identify yarns of a certain weight or category. Never fear. There are some tips and tricks you can use to identify lace weight yarns with certainty.

The first, and most obvious, approach is to look for the CYC symbol that looks like this:

The entire point of creating those industry-wide symbols (they look like teeny skeins with numbers in them) is to establish a uniform way to indicate yarn category. Most larger yarn manufacturers in the US place the CYC symbol somewhere on their labels. If you see a yarn marked as Category 0 – Lace, then it's lace weight yarn.

If the yarn you're considering doesn't contain the CYC symbol, don't despair. Generally speaking, you can determine a yarn's category by comparing the yardage contained in the skein to the skein's weight. A one-pound cone of lace weight yarn tends to have somewhere between 3000 and 6000 yards in it. That means a 25g skein of lace weight will contain 165 to

330 yards of yarn; a 50g skein will contain 330 to 660 yards; and so on (remember that these are ranges, so there will be some minor variations in the exact number of yards[2]).

Weight	Yardage
25g	150 to 330 yds
50g	330 to 660 yds
100g	660 to 1300+ yds
1 lb.	3000 to 6000 yds

Still feeling unsure whether you've got the right stuff?

- Check the suggested gauge listed on the yarn label. If a suggested gauge is given and your yarn is indeed lace weight, the gauge will either (a) call for 8 or more stitches per inch and a very small needle (such as a 0 or 1); or (b) state that gauge varies, and give a wide range of suggested needle sizes (e.g., "size 3 to 8") and gauges (e.g., "4 to 8 sts per inch").
- Sounds obvious, but take a look at the name of the yarn. Often the word "lace" will appear in the name of the yarn (for example, "Rowan Fine Lace"); lace weight yarns are also sometimes described as two-ply (especially British and Australian yarns), cobweb, or thread.
- Ask for advice from a knowledgeable sales clerk or a trusted knitting pal. Or use an internet search engine to find out more about the yarn you're considering.

What is a WPI?

You may run across references to "WPI" or "wraps per inch." The WPI system is an alternative way to classify yarn categories, often used by handspinners to measure their handspun yarns. The WPI system measures how many times a strand of yarn can be wrapped around a one-inch increment of an item like a ruler. The number of wraps in one inch is compared to a standard range to determine what category the yarn is.

I find the wraps-per-inch system to be less than ideal for two reasons: first, it's hard to be sure that everyone wraps their yarn the same way. How tightly yarn is wrapped and how closely the strands sit next to each other can greatly affect the number of strands that will fit into a one-inch space. With those variables, the WPI system becomes much less effective as a standard system of measurement. Another problem I've encountered when trying to work with WPI ratios are the wildly divergent ranges given for the same category of yarn depending on which resource one consults. For example, when researching this book, I found various sources identifying lace weight yarn as having 18 or more WPI, 32 to 40 WPI and 30+ WPI. Clear as mud, right?

If I'm unsure what category a yarn falls into, and I can't figure it out from online research, I prefer to use the yardage of a skein relative to weight as a general guideline and let swatching tell me the rest.

[2] If the skein lists yardage but not weight, use a postal or food scale to weigh it. If you don't own one, you might ask the clerk at your local Post Office really, really nicely if you can use his or hers.

Tips for Working With Coned Yarn

Have you ever been tempted to purchase coned yarn, perhaps while browsing at a store that sells weaving as well as knitting supplies? Most companies that produce yarns specifically marketed for knitting and crochet sell them in smaller quantities weighing 50 or 100 grams, but yarns sold as weaving yarns often are sold in cones holding one pound or more of the yarn. Many coned yarns are perfectly suitable for knitting, and may offer tremendous value or the chance to knit with a less-common fiber or blend of fibers. (And fewer ends to weave in at the end is another bonus.)

If you're lucky, the shop where you're browsing will include approximate knitting gauge for these enticing coned yarns, or will at least give you a general sense for what category the yarn falls into (e.g., the description of the yarn will say something like "knits as a sportweight yarn"). Sometimes, however, instead of a descriptor like "worsted weight" or an approximate number of stitches per inch, the cone is labeled with a fraction, like "8/2" or "2/10." What do those numbers mean? And how can you predict the approximate gauge if you were to knit that coned yarn?

Figuring out the fraction for a coned yarn can be a little tricky. Different manufacturers put the numbers in the fraction in a different order; Mill A might label a yarn as "8/2" while Mill B might switch the order of the numbers in the fraction and label the same yarn "2/8." And my friends at WEBS—America's Yarn Store put the numbers in one order for wool yarns, and the reverse for cotton and linen.

Generally, however, one of the numbers in the fraction represents the number of plies (constituent strands) that particular yarn has. For example, the Colrain Lace used for one of the lovely projects in this book is labeled as "2/10" with the "2" meaning it's a two-ply yarn—two strands are wrapped around each other to create the finished yarn.

The other number in the fraction is a little more complicated and has to do with the number of yards in a pound of that yarn. Each specific kind of yarn—cotton, linen, wool—is sized based on the number of yards of one ply of that yarn contained in a pound. For example, a typical skein of one-ply cotton yarn has 840 yards per pound; a typical skein of one-ply worsted wool yarn contains 560 yards; and so on. The second number in the fraction is a multiplier based on the standard number of yards per pound. In our example above, the Colrain Lace has a multiplier of 10, meaning that there are 10 x the standard number of single-ply yards per pound (10 x 560 yards per pound = 5600 is the basic count for this particular yarn), or 5600 single-ply yards per pound. Divide by the number of plies to get final yardage per pound: 5600 divided by 2 plies = 2800 two-ply yards per pound. Once you know that number of yards per pound, you can compare this to a table of yards per pound by category.

For most knitters, when experimenting with coned yarns, it makes sense to find a knowledgeable salesperson to give a better sense of the yarn's category and weight, or do some internet sleuthing to see if other knitters have posted their experiences with a particular yarn.

tools of the trade

IF YOU'RE NEW TO FINE-GAUGE YARNS, play it smart. Begin your lace weight journey by thinking about the yarn and tools that are right for you and your project.

Let's start with yarn choice. I'll talk a bit more about yarn substitution later, but as a general rule, if you're a new knitter or haven't knit with many fine-gauge yarns, opt for yarns that are solid, light-colored, and smooth for best success.

Why? Light-colored yarns are easier to see than darker ones, and solid yarns are less distracting than multi-colored ones. For the same reason, yarns that have a lot of texture—yarns with a fuzzy rather than smooth surface, say, or novelty yarns like boucles—can be trickier to handle than yarns that are smooth. It's harder to get even stitches with textured yarns, and the halo from loose fibers or the decorative pieces on some art yarns can be distracting. (Not that I have anything against these kinds of yarns, mind you, but for your first foray into fine yarns, best to stick to yarns that are easier to work with.) So put down that ball of navy-blue mohair boucle! At least for now.

Fiber choice—exactly what your yarn is made from—can also make a difference in your first foray into lightweight yarns. Wool or wool-blend yarns can't be beat when you're just starting out since wool fibers have bounce and elasticity. As the needle moves through each stitch, yarns with wool content stretch a little and then snap back, making the knitting process more enjoyable. It's easier to get a consistent gauge with a more elastic yarn, and any stitch manipulation—whether increases or decreases, cables or twisted stitches—will be more pleasant. While plant fibers like cotton, linen and silk have many delightful qualities, they tend to be less forgiving and more slippery than wool and wool-blend yarns. Their inherent inelasticity may add undue stress when you're just getting used to fine-gauge yarns.

Once you've selected an appropriate yarn, it's time to consider the needles you're going to put that yarn on. Check the pattern to see if it calls for circular or straight needles. Many knitters have developed preferences for one or the other, but when it comes to knitting with superfine yarns, there are times when the number of stitches needed for a project require the knitter to use a circular rather than a straight needle. Straight needles range in length, but very rarely come in lengths greater than, say, 14 or 16 inches long. If you're knitting a garment with a relatively large number of cast-on stitches, those stitches simply may not fit on a straight needle. Even if you could fit them all, many knitters find it more comfortable to spread out a large number of stitches over the cable of a circular needle, distributing the stitches over a wider distance to reduce weight and pressure on the hands.

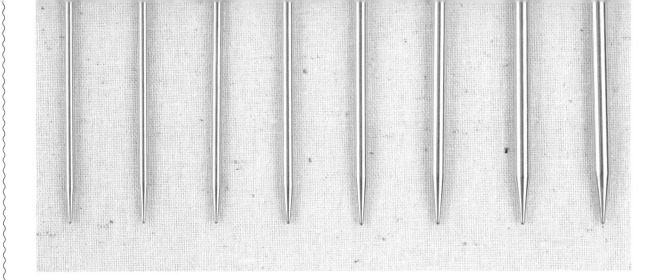

If you're using circular needles, make sure you take a good look at the join, the place where the cable is attached to the needle shafts. Some knitting needles have extremely smooth, seamless joins, while others have joins that are less smooth and more bulky. For best results, opt for the former. No one wants to tug or fiddle with stitches that don't slide easily over the join.

Whether you'll be using straight or circular needles, the surface of the needle is another important consideration. Today's knitter gets to choose from an astonishing variety of materials when it comes to knitting needles: metal (some with special coatings), glass, wood, bamboo, plastic, casein, carbon, and more. While some of it boils down to personal preference, most knitters agree that what a knitting needle is made of can affect its performance. Metal, especially metal with slick coatings, like the Addi Turbo needles, is fastest and slipperiest: stitches glide quickly across the surface of the needle. Wood, bamboo, and plastic have some "grip" so that stitches move more slowly. If you're finding that the

stitches fly too quickly over your needle, making your knitting feel out of control, switching to a "stickier" surface, like bamboo, may help slow you down and feel more comfortable.

While we're on the subject of needle surfaces, here's a tip from the great designer Fiona Ellis. She recommends thinking about the color of the needle relative to the color of the yarn you'll be using. For best visibility, make sure there's contrast between the color of the yarn and the color of the needle shaft. If your knitting needles have a black surface, best not to cast on a black yarn, as you'll go crazy trying to discern where the stitches begin and end.

Last consideration when it comes to needles is the tip. Some knitting needles are designed to have sharp, narrow tips; others have more rounded, blunter tips. When knitting with superfine yarn, sharper thinner tips slide more readily into stitches and make manipulating stitches easier. Some knitting needles are even designed with finer-gauge yarns in mind, and are marketed as especially suited for lace or sock knitting for that reason (for example, Addi Lace needles). I am frequently surprised at how drastically the shape of a needle tip can affect the pleasure I take in knitting a fine-gauge yarn. If I'm struggling to get even tension or finding it hard to slide the needle into the individual stitches, a switch to a sharper point can make all the difference in the world.

tips for intrepid knitting

AS MY MOM LIKES TO SAY, "There are tricks to every trade." And there are certain tips and techniques that can help you manage your superfine knitting a bit better. Here are several that I've compiled, with the help of my knitting friends.

- Lighting. Sounds almost too easy, but making sure you've got sufficiently bright light can make a big difference when you're working with thinner yarn and (in some cases) a relatively large number of stitches. Natural light, the kind that streams through a window, is ideal; many knitters swear by their full-spectrum lights for working in the evening or when it's cloudy.

- Project choice is important, too. If knitting with thinner yarn feels awkward, start with a simple and relatively small project, like the Square in the Round Poncho or the Coaxial Baby Cap. You'll have a chance to get your hands used to holding fine yarn and manipulating skinnier stitches. As you get accustomed to the process of knitting fine, branch out to projects with more elaborate stitch patterns, like cables or eyelets.

- Yarn handling. After you've picked your project but before you cast on, take a good look at your ball or hank of yarn. Remember that superfine yarns are more delicate than thicker yarns, so if you need to wind a center-pull ball (often called a yarn "cake") from a hank, you'll want to be extra-careful not to break the yarn. Don't jerk the yarn and don't go too fast if you're using a ballwinder and swift. I find that it can help to loosen the tension of the swift arms just a tiny bit to allow the swift to turn more readily.

- If you're using a prewound skein, take a good look to see if the yarn is firmly wound or if it needs rewinding. This is especially true for slippery yarns; I have been reduced to tears when a soft, supple silk yarn has slid out of its original shape and slithered its way into a tangled mess. If you anticipate slippage, you may want to rewind an especially slick yarn onto a piece of cardboard. Although I don't tend to use them on a regular basis, if your yarn is particularly sticky or slippery, a yarn "bra" or other type of cover (a clean knee-high stocking will work, as will a portion of an unwound shower pouf) can help you avoid tangles.

- Cast-on methods. I'm a long tail cast-on girl, myself, but working with thinner yarns has made me rethink my method of casting on from time to time. As a practical matter, it can be tough to estimate exactly how long a tail one needs to cast on, say, 257 stitches. (And nothing is worse than having just enough yarn to cast on 255 or 256 of those stitches, then having to rip it all out and start counting again.) But I've learned a lot from my talented knitting friends and one of the best things I learned from lace maven Brooke Nico was the

utility of the knitted-on cast-on. You don't need a long tail, and it provides you with a much looser set of edge stitches. Those looser edge stitches can help make blocking a project a breeze.

✖ Stitch markers. One of my favorite tips (and not just for working with superfine yarns) is the judicious use of stitch markers. A set or two of stitch markers in a variety of colors is an inexpensive and easy way to help speed your knitting along and prevent the need for ripping out inches and inches of work. Stitch markers can help you right from the start, with your cast-on. Pop a stitch marker on every, say, 50 stitches, making your final count much easier. Stitch markers can also help you keep track of repeats when working across a long row or round. Place a stitch marker after every or every other repeat, so you'll spot any mistakes long before the end of the row or round. Or set off edging stitches at the beginning and end of a row with markers so you'll never forget to work them in the appropriate stitch pattern.

✖ Chart-reading. You'll notice that many of the patterns in this book use charted stitch patterns. Using charts is a terrific way to visualize what your knitting should look like and to recognize mistakes before you get too far along. If you're like me and your eyes aren't what they used to be, try enlarging your charts on a photocopier to make them easier to read. Some knitters use highlighters to mark up their charts, color-coding them to make them easier to read (e.g. highlighting all yarnovers in blue, all k2tog's in yellow, etc.). It also helps to use some sort of mechanism to keep track of rows. Removable sticky notes or tape are helpful for this; you can also find metal stands with magnetic strips that are designed especially for keeping track of knitting charts (you may find them along with cross-stitching supplies).

✖ Stay cool. Perhaps the most important tip I can give you: don't panic. Lace weight yarns in particular require a good blocking to achieve their full beauty. It can be intimidating to knit along and produce something that looks like a limp dishrag, but if you've knit and blocked a swatch (which I highly recommend you do for so many reasons!) you'll at least have a tangible reminder that the project that looks droopy and lifeless as it comes off the needles will magically turn into airy, even mesh or crisp eyelets when properly blocked. Honest.

Lifelines

In the dog-eat-dog world of yarn, knitters can disagree about just anything—even about something as beneficial-sounding as a "lifeline." If you aren't familiar with the term, it refers to a very thin piece of thread, ribbon, or yarn (some aficionados swear by dental floss) threaded through a row or round of stitches, particularly when knitting lace. The lifeline serves as a back-up: if you make a mistake and need to unravel stitches, you can use the lifeline to avoid having to rip the entire work out. Just unravel the stitches until you get to the lifeline row—and use the lifeline to help you replace the stitches on your needle, letting it guide you stitch by stitch. Lifelines are traditionally used in hardcore lace knitting, where it can be diabolically easy to drop a stitch or miss an increase or decrease. Knitters who use lifelines periodically thread them through a row or round (it's easiest to place them in a row that is all knit stitches) so they have a kind of insurance as they go along. Of course there's no reason why lifelines can't be used in any kind of knitting, whether a lacy stitch or not, so if you like the idea of having a back-up plan, you may find a lifeline useful. I sometimes wonder if the existence of the lifeline relaxes you enough to avoid making as many mistakes.

That being said, I have knitting friends who create copious amounts of gorgeous lacework without ever using a lifeline. These knitters feel that it's more important to learn how to read the stitches you're knitting so that you can see a mistake as soon as it happens (and hopefully fix it right away), rather than continuing on, row after row, without noticing your mistakes, only to have to rip back later.

don't be a blockhead!

I'VE ALREADY MENTIONED the seemingly-miraculous process of blocking. However, blocking is so important that I'm going to mention it again. Whether you're knitting with thick or thin yarns, blocking is one of the most important things you can do to improve the finished appearance of your knitting. Blocking helps even out your stitches and blend in minor imperfections and mistakes. If you're knitting at a looser-than-typical gauge, or doing eyelets or other decorative stitchwork, blocking is essential to get the full effect of all your hard work—it makes the pattern pop.

There are as many methods for blocking as there are knitters, but the essential steps involve soaking your knitting in tepid water, gently using a towel to remove excess water by blotting, then using pins, wires, or a combination of both to stretch out the knitting and coax it into the desired shape. Some pieces will require very vigorous blocking while others will only need to be shaped and smoothed. There are some excellent video tutorials on the web if you're not sure what to do. Just don't skip this step!

on yarn substitution

AS I'VE MENTIONED BEFORE, lace weight yarns come in an almost infinite variety of styles, fibers, colors, and constructions. When the contributing designers and I selected yarns for the projects in this book, we tried to give you a kind of "Best of Lace Yarns" list—tried and true workhorses, new favorites, different fibers and textures, yarns from small companies and yarns from big ones. We certainly hope you'll give them a try!

If you'd like to use yarn from your stash or can't find the sample yarns for some reason (every so often a yarn gets discontinued and breaks our collective hearts), rest assured that you'll find lots of great choices that you can use in the projects in this book. The most important thing to remember is to stick with a Category 0/lace yarn (see pp. 11). All yarns in this category have approximately the same weight and knit at roughly the same gauge. You may have to do some quick math to make sure you buy the same total number of yards, but if you stay within the Category 0/lace yarn category, you'll be unlikely to encounter any gauge problems that you can't solve by tweaking needle size.

If you're still uncomfortable picking a substitute yarn, ease into the process by sticking with the same brand and type of yarn, but opting for a different color. Or pick a substitute yarn that is similar in appearance to the sample yarn: look for similar fiber content (e.g., substitute a merino wool for a merino wool), similar yarn construction (e.g., if the original yarn is a single ply, pick a single-ply substitute) and similar color effects (e.g., find another yarn with slowly morphing stripes to substitute for the one in the sample).

Don't forget about the folks at your local yarn shop or knitting group– there's usually plenty of fiber-loving folk there who will help consider the pros and cons of various yarn choices and tell you about their experiences with specific yarns. And the internet is chock-full of resources that can help you make good yarn choices. For example, the pattern search function on the website www.Ravelry.com allows you to search a specific pattern and see who else has made it; scrolling through other folks' versions of a project is a great way to judge how well a particular yarn works. Likewise, Ravelry's yarn search function provides plenty of feedback from actual knitters and crocheters about a specific yarn's performance. Even using a search engine to look up the name of a specific yarn can yield useful information about how it performs on the needle from bloggers, chat rooms, and yarn review websites.

NOT ALL SKEINS ARE CREATED EQUAL

In my previous book, *Sock Yarn Studio*, we divided the patterns into sections based on the number of skeins of sock yarn they required. This was easy to do with sock yarn, as it is generally sold in units of around 400 yards/380m, give or take—the amount necessary to knit

an average-sized pair of socks. A one-skein project took 400 yards or less, a two-skein project took between 400 and 800 yards, and so on. Knitters (and LYS owners!) responded so well to this system that we wanted to use it in this book, too. However, there's one wrinkle.

Unlike skeins of sock yarn, which pretty consistently measure around 400 yards over 100g, skeins of lace weight yarn vary appreciably in yardage. For example, looking at just a few of the yarns used in this book: one skein of Lotus Yarns Mimi contains 330 yards; one skein of Black Bunny Fibers Heavenly Lace contains a whopping 1300 yards; and a skein of Rowan Kidsilk Haze contains 229 yards. Quite a difference.

Just to make things even more confusing, not all of the projects take an entire skein of yarn. For example, a specific lace weight yarn may be sold only in skeins of 1300 yards, while the actual pattern takes significantly less than that amount. If you were purchasing a substitute yarn, you wouldn't need to purchase the equivalent of 1300 yards—you could purchase a smaller hank and still be confident you'd have enough yarn.

To keep you from going crazy, we've grouped the projects by yardage and approximate number of skeins.

The first pattern section includes designs which use about one skein (up to 400 yards) of lace weight yarn, all of which is in the same color. Designs in the second section require between 400 and 900 yards of lace weight yarn in the same color, or two different colors of lace weight yarn, and the last section contains designs that use more than 3 colors or require more than 900 yards of lace weight yarn. Note that we've included more exact estimates of yardage for each pattern to give you a sense of exactly how much of the listed yarn was used when knitting the sample. You'll also see that a handful of patterns combine lace weight yarns with a yarn that is heavier; for example, the Eden Scarf uses a lace weight yarn in a solid color, and a sock/fingering weight yarn in a contrasting multicolor. We've assigned those patterns categories based solely on the amount of lace weight yarn they use.

It's always important to check yardage requirements for any pattern you're about to make, but it's especially important when using lace weight yarns, where yardage and weight can vary so wildly from skein to skein. So please do read the pattern requirements carefully before purchasing yarn or casting on.

Color effects in lace weight yarn

One of the most delightful aspects of lace weight yarn is the variety of color effects they can contain. But that can make it confusing when it comes time for selecting yarns. Here's a quick guide to some of the most common types of yarns you'll see, along with tips for where and how to use them.

- Solid and semisolid yarns. This category includes undyed yarns, yarns that are dyed in solid colors by machine, and that are handdyed in one or mostly one color. Solids and semisolids were used in the Blue Diamond Scarf, the Mihika Cardigan and the Récherché Vest and Scarf. These yarns are the most versatile: they can be used in any pattern successfully, but are particularly useful for more complicated stitch patterns. The uniformity of the color keeps the focus on your stitchwork rather than the color changes of the yarn.

- Multicolored yarns. This category includes multicolored handpaints and yarns that are machine-dyed in multiple colors. The Graciela Pullover uses a multicolored yarn along with two semisolids, and the seed stitch panels of the Eden Scarf use a multicolored fingering weight yarn. The general rule-of-thumb when it comes to colored yarns is that either the yarn does the work or the knitter does the work. Multicolored yarns tend to look better knit in simpler patterns, so the yarn won't overshadow the stitchwork.

- Striping or graduated-color yarns. Some yarns are specially constructed, either by dyeing or plying, to create stripes, either fairly delineated stripes or the kind that slowly morph from one color to the next. The Plied Stripes Sweater uses a slowly-striping yarn in tonal shades of red to give subtle color shifts.

One
SKEIN
PROJECTS

A Little Luxe Gauntlets

DESIGN BY Andi Smith SKILL LEVEL: Intermediate

The glamour of Old Hollywood comes together with mink to create a modern twist on lady-gloves. Taking just one skein to create, these gloves are an affordable touch of luxury that will become timeless classics.

FINISHED MEASUREMENTS
Fits ladies' medium-size hand

MATERIALS AND TOOLS
Lotus Yarns Mimi (100% mink; 1.75oz/50g = 330yd/301m): 1 skein, color gray #04—approx 300yd/274m of lace weight yarn

Knitting needles: Two 2.75mm (size 2 U.S.) 32"/80cm circular needles or size to obtain gauge

2 dpns in size above (for creating pleats)

Stitch markers

Tapestry needle

Stitch holder or waste yarn

Fourteen ¼"/6mm buttons

GAUGE
32 sts/40 rnds = 4"/10cm in St st

Always take time to check your gauge.

SPECIAL ABBREVIATIONS
Cdd (Centered double decrease) – Slip 2 sts as if to k2tog, k1, p2sso.

Kfb (knit into front and back) – Knit into the front and back of the next stitch.

Pbf (purl into back and front) – Purl into the back and front of the next stitch.

LFP (Left Facing Pleat) – Slip next 2 sts onto first dpn, slip following 2 sts onto 2nd dpn, turn the 2nd dpn 180 degrees clockwise, so that it is lying in front of the first 2 sts on the left-hand needle, lay the first dpn on top of the 2nd dpn so that you have 3 layers of sts facing you, with the first dpn on top. Knit the first st of each needle together (3 sts tog) 2 times. You will have 2 sts rem from the original 6 in the pleat.

RFP (Right Facing Pleat) – Slip the next 2 sts onto first dpn, slip the following 2 sts onto 2nd dpn, turn the 2nd dpn 180 degrees counterclockwise so that it is lying behind the first 2 sts on the left-hand needle, lay the first dpn behind the 2nd dpn, so that you have 3 layers of sts with the left-hand needle sitting on top. Knit the first st of each needle together (3 sts tog) 2 times. You will have 2 sts rem from the original 6 in the pleat.

3-st wrap – With yarn in back, slip next 3 sts to right-hand needle, bring yarn from back to front, slip 3 sts back to left-hand needle, and k1-tbl, p1, k1-tbl.

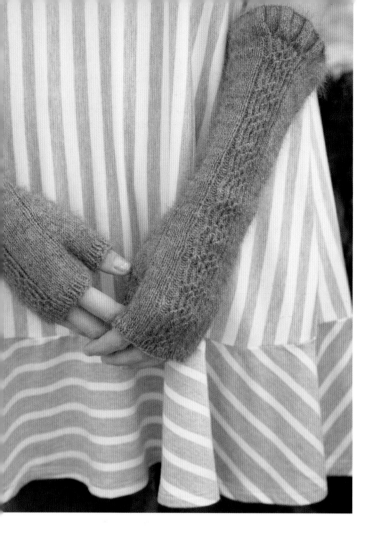

Row 9: Rep Row 5.

Row 11: Rep Row 3.

Row 12: Rep Row 2.

Rep these 12 rows.

Chart B worked in rnds (over 13 sts):

Rnd 1 (RS): [P1, k1-tbl] 6 times, k1.

Rnd 2 and all WS rnds: [P1, p1-tbl] 6 times, k1.

Rnd 3: [P1, k1-tbl] twice, p1, 3-st wrap, [p1, k1-tbl] twice, k1.

Rnd 5: P1, k1-tbl, [p1, 3-st wrap] twice, p1, k1-tbl, k1.

Rnd 7: [P1, 3-st wrap] 3 times, k1.

Rnd 9: Rep Row 5.

Rnd 11: Rep Row 3.

Rnd 12: Rep Row 2.

Rep these 12 rnds.

Chart C worked in rnds (beg over 11 sts):

Rnd 1 (RS): [P1, k1-tbl] 5 times, p1.

Rnd 2: Rep Rnd 1.

Rnd 3: P1, k1-tbl, p1, ssk, k1-tbl, k2tog, p1, k-1tbl, p1—9 sts.

Rnd 4: [P1, k1-tbl] twice, k1-tbl, [k1-tbl, p1] twice.

Rnd 5: P1, k1-tbl, p1, cdd, p1, k1-tbl, p1—7 sts.

Rnd 6: [P1, k1-tbl] 3 times, p1.

Rnd 7: P1, ssk, k1-tbl, k2tog, p1—5 sts.

Rnd 8: P1, [k1-tbl] 3 times, p1.

Rnd 9: P1, cdd, p1—3 sts.

Rnd 10: P1, k1-tbl, p1.

Rnd 11: Cdd—1 st.

Rnd 12: K1.

Rep these 12 rnds.

Notes: Work begins at upper arm end of gauntlet and is worked back and forth in rows on one circular needle.

PATTERN STITCHES

Chart A worked in rows (over 5 sts):

Row 1 (RS): [P1, k1-tbl] twice, p1.

Row 2: [K1, p1-tbl] twice, k1.

Row 3: P1, 3-st wrap, p1.

Row 4: Rep Row 2.

Rep these 4 rows.

Chart B worked in rows (over 13 sts):

Row 1 (RS): [P1, k1-tbl] 6 times, k1.

Row 2 and all WS rows: P1, [p1-tbl, k1] 6 times.

Row 3: [P1, k1-tbl] twice, p1, 3-st wrap, [p1, k1-tbl] twice, k1.

Row 5: P1, k1-tbl, [p1, 3-st wrap] twice, p1, k1-tbl, k1.

Row 7: [P1, 3-st wrap] 3 times, k1.

After buttoned opening is complete, work is joined and worked in rnds to hand end of gauntlet. Use 2 circular needles to work in rnds or, if desired, use a set of double-pointed needles.

INSTRUCTIONS

Using long-tail method, CO 106 sts.

Foundation Row (WS): [K1, p1-tbl] twice, k1, p16, pm, p14, [p2, k2, p4, k2, p2] 3 times, p14, pm, p16, [k1, p1-tbl] twice, k1.

Slip markers as you come to them.

Row 1 (RS): Work Row 1 of Chart A, k30, [k2, p2, k4, p2, k2] 3 times, k30, work Row 1 of Chart A.

Row 2: Work Row 2 of Chart A, p30, [p2, k2, p4, k2, p2] 3 times, p30, work Row 2 of Chart A.

Row 3: Work Row 3 of Chart A, k30, [k2, p2, k4, p2, k2] 3 times, k30, work Row 3 of Chart A.

Row 4: Work Row 4 of Chart A, p30, [p2, k2, p4, k2, p2] 3 times, p30, work Row 4 of Chart A.

Rows 5–7: Rep Rows 1–3.

Row 8 (buttonhole row—WS): [K the first st, place it back on left-hand needle] 3 times, work across row in patt as established.

Rows 9 and 10: Work in patt as established.

Row 11 (dec row): [Work in patt as established to 4 sts before first marker, k2tog, k2, sl marker, k2, ssk] twice, work in patt as established to end of row—102 sts.

Rows 12–14: Work in patt as established.

Row 15 (pleat row): Work Chart A over 5 sts, k28, [RFP, LFP] 3 times, k28, work Chart A over 5 sts—78 sts rem.

Row 16: [K the first st, place it back on left-hand needle] 3 times, work Chart A over first 5 sts, p to first marker, sl marker, p19, pbf, p to last 5 sts, work Chart A over 5 sts—79 sts.

Row 17: Work Chart A over first 5 sts, k to first marker, sl marker, k13, work Chart B over next 13 sts, k to last 5 sts, work Chart A over last 5 sts.

Rows 18–20: Work in patt as established.

Row 21: Rep Row 11 (dec row)—75 sts.

Continue to work in patt as established, and continue to rep buttonhole row every 8th row (i.e., Row 24, 32, etc.) 4 more times and dec row every 10th row (i.e., Rows 21, 31, etc.) 4 more times—59 sts rem.

Row 62: Work in patt as established.

Note: Work now proceeds in rnds.

Rnd 63: Break yarn, remove markers, and join in the rnd by slipping sts to first marker onto one needle, slip sts between markers onto 2nd needle, and rem sts onto first needle—30 sts on needle 1, 29 sts on needle 2.

Rnd 64: K10, p1, [k1-tbl, p1] twice, pbf, [k1-tbl, p1] twice, work in patt as established to end of rnd—60 sts (31 sts on needle 1, 29 sts on needle 2).

Rnd 65: K10, work Chart C across next 11 sts, work in patt as established to end of rnd.

Continue working in patt as established until Chart C has been completed—50 sts.

Work 10 rnds without shaping keeping continuity of Chart B in the center of needle 2.

Thumb Gusset:

Prepare to work thumb gusset by placing a stitch marker after the 3rd st on needle 1 for the right-hand glove and after the 18th st on needle 1 for the left-hand glove.

Rnd 76: Work to marker, sl marker, kfb, place another marker, work to end of rnd as established—51 sts (2 sts between markers).

Rnd 77: Work in patt as established.

Rnd 78: Work to marker, sl marker, [kfb] twice, sl marker, work to end of rnd as established—53 sts (4 sts between markers).

Rnd 79: Work in patt as established.

Rnd 80: Work to marker, sl marker, kfb, work to 1 st before next marker, kfb, sl marker, work to end of rnd as established—55 sts (6 sts between markers).

Rnds 81–96: Rep Rnds 79 and 80 until there are 22 sts between the stitch markers—71 sts total.

Rnd 97: Work to first marker, remove marker, slip the 22 thumb gusset sts to waste yarn or stitch holder, CO 7 sts, remove remaining marker, and work remainder of rnd as established—56 sts total.

Rnd 98: Work in patt as established.

Continue working without shaping, and keeping the continuity of Chart B, work another 2½"/6cm or so, until when tried on, the glove just reaches the tip of your knuckles, ending on Rnd 1, 2, or 12 of Chart B.

Rib:

Next rnd: Knit to beg of the chart sts, pm, this is now new beg of rnd.

Rnds 1–3: *P1, k1-tbl; rep from * to end of rnd.

Rnd 4: [P1, k1-tbl] twice, p1, 3 st-wrap *p1, k1-tbl; rep from * to end of rnd.

Rnds 5–7: Rep Rnd 1.

BO in patt.

Thumb:

Pick up the 22 sts from waste yarn or stitch holder, CO 4 sts (to be sewn to the 7-st hand cast-on later) or pick up 4 sts across the 7-st hand cast-on—26 sts.

Work 1"/2.5cm in St st.

Rib:

Rnd 1: [K2tog] twice, *p1, k1-tbl; rep from * to end of rnd—24 sts.

Rnds 2–4: [P1, k1-tbl], repeat to end of rnd.

BO in patt.

FINISHING

Weave in all ends securely.

Attach buttons to correspond with buttonholes.

Wet block, being sure to pin the pleats into place until fully dry.

Note: If thumb stitches were added by casting on stitches rather than by picking up stitches from gusset, sew cast-on edge to mitten to eliminate hole.

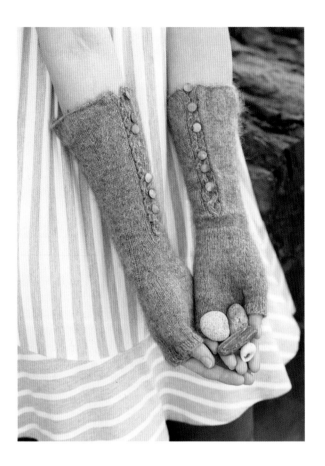

Chart A

	5	4	3	2	1	
4	●	B	●	B	●	
	●	<	●	>	●	3
2	●	B	●	B	●	
	●	B	●	B	●	1

Chart B

Chart B is worked both flat and in the round. When working rounds, read every row from right to left. When working flat, read RS rows from right to left and WS rows from left to right.

	13	12	11	10	9	8	7	6	5	4	3	2	1	
12	B	●	B	●	B	●	B	●	B	●	B	●		12
11	B	●	B	●	<	●	>	●	B	●	B	●		11
10	B	●	B	●	B	●	B	●	B	●	B	●		10
9	B	●	<	●	>	●	<	●	>	●	B	●		9
8	B	●	B	●	B	●	B	●	B	●	B	●		8
7	<	●	>	●	<	●	>	●	<	●	>	●		7
6	B	●	B	●	B	●	B	●	B	●	B	●		6
5	B	●	<	●	>	●	<	●	>	●	B	●		5
4	B	●	B	●	B	●	B	●	B	●	B	●		4
3	B	●	B	●	<	●	>	●	B	●	B	●		3
2	B	●	B	●	B	●	B	●	B	●	B	●		2
1	B	●	B	●	B	●	B	●	B	●	B	●		1

Chart C

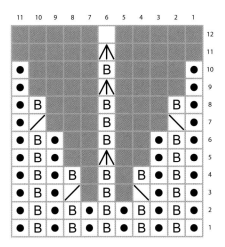

Key

● **Purl**
Purl Stitch.

B **Knit-tbl**
k1-tbl on RS and p1-tbl on WS.

☐ **Knit**
Knit Stitch.

< ● > **3-st wrap**
Slip next 3 sts to RH needle, bring yarn from back to front, slip the 3 sts back to LH needle, then k1-tbl, p1, k1-tbl.

╲ **SSK**
Slip 1 stitch as if to knit. Slip another stitch as if to knit. Insert LH needle into front of these 2 stitches and knit them together.

▨ **No Stitch**
Placeholder—No stitch made.

╱ **K2tog**
Knit 2 stitches together as 1 stitch.

⋏ **Central double decrease**
Slip first and second stitches together as if to knit. Knit 1 stitch. Pass 2 slipped stitches over the knit stitch.

Wind on the Water Scarf

DESIGNER: Barbara J. Brown SKILL LEVEL: Easy

A series of mini-cables adds movement and texture to this beautiful scarf. We chose to give this one a very light steam blocking, to retain the crinkly texture of the knitted fabric that so perfectly evokes the feeling of wind ruffling the ocean waves.

FINISHED MEASUREMENTS
Approx 72"/183cm by 8"/20cm

MATERIALS AND TOOLS
Ancient Arts Fibres British BFL Lace (100% superwash Bluefaced Leicester wool; 3.5oz/100g = 874yd/800m): 1 skein, color Corfu—approx 435yd/398m of lace weight yarn (0)

Knitting needles: 6mm (size 10 U.S.) or size to obtain gauge

Cable needle

Tapestry needle

GAUGE
24 sts/28 rows = 4"/10cm in Garter st

Always take time to check your gauge.

SPECIAL ABBREVIATION
C12B – Place 6 sts on cn, hold in back of work, k next 6 sts, k 6 sts from cn.

PATTERN STITCHES
Picot Cast-On: *Using knit cast-on method, CO 5 sts. BO 2 sts, then sl rem st from right needle to left needle; rep from * until desired number of sts rem on needle.

Picot Bind-Off: *Using knit cast-on method, CO 2 sts to left needle. BO 5 sts in the usual way, then sl rem st from right needle to left needle; rep from * to end, then fasten off rem st.

INSTRUCTIONS

Scarf:

Using Picot Cast-On, CO 42 sts, then CO an additional 2 sts in the usual way—44 sts.

Rows 1–20: Sl 1 purlwise wyif, k to end.

Note: Continue to slip first st purlwise wyif.

Row 21 (RS): Sl 1, k5, C12B, k26.

Rows 22–30: Sl 1, k to end.

Row 31 (RS): Sl 1, k25, C12B, k6.

Rows 32–40: Sl 1, k to end.

Row 41 (RS): Sl 1, k15, C12B, k16.

Rows 42–50: Sl 1, k to end.

Row 51 (RS): Sl 1, k15, C12B, k16.

Rows 52–60: Sl 1, k to end.

Row 61 (RS): Sl 1, k5, C12B, k26.

Rows 62–70: Sl 1, k to end.

Row 71 (RS): Sl 1, k5, C12B, k8, C12B, k6.

Rows 72–80: Sl 1, k to end.

Row 81 (RS): Sl 1, k25, C12B, k6.

Rows 82–90: Sl 1, k to end.

Row 91 (RS): Sl 1, k15, C12B, k16.

Rows 92–100: Sl 1, k to end.

Rep Rows 21–100 five more times.

Next 10 rows: Sl 1, k to end.

BO all sts using Picot Bind- Off.

FINISHING

Weave in ends.

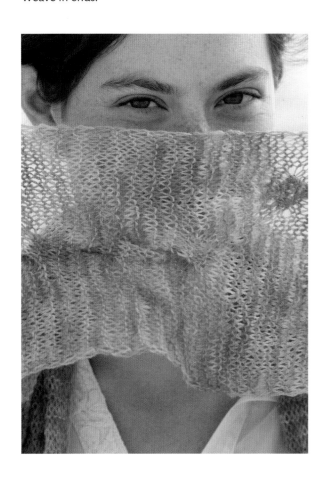

Taleya Pillow Cover

DESIGNER: Carol J. Sulcoski SKILL LEVEL: Easy

Lace and pillowcovers go together like chocolate-chip cookies and milk.

But I wondered what would happen if instead of using lace ruffles for edging,

I knit the entire front of the pillow in a decidedly unfloral pattern, using a

bold, rich color, and set it off with a plush velveteen fabric backing.

I loved the result and hope you do, too!

FINISHED MEASUREMENTS
Approx 16"/41cm square

MATERIALS AND TOOLS
Lorna's Laces Helen's Lace (50% tussah silk/50% merino; 4oz/113g = 1250yd/1143m): 1 skein, color Patina—approx 250yd/229m of lace weight yarn (0)

Knitting needles: 3.75mm (size 5 U.S.) or size to obtain gauge

Stitch marker (optional)

Tapestry needle

Approx ½yd/0.5m of fabric in each of two colors for pillow underlay and backing

Sewing needle and thread

16"/40cm pillow form

GAUGE
20sts/24 rows = 4"/10cm in Lace Stitch Pattern, after blocking

Always take time to check your gauge.

SPECIAL ABBREVIATION
Sk2p – Slip next 2 sts tog knitwise; knit next st; pass 2 slipped sts over knit st—2 sts dec.

PATTERN STITCH

Lace Stitch Pattern (multiple of 3 sts):

Row 1 (RS): *Sk2p, yo twice, rep from * to end.

Row 2: *[P1 then k1 into double yo], p1, rep from * to end.

Row 3: Knit.

Row 4: Rep Row 1.

Row 5: Rep Row 2.

Row 6: Knit.

INSTRUCTIONS

CO 82 sts.

Beg with a K row, work 6 rows in St st.

Switch to Lace Stitch Patt as follows:

Row 1 (RS): K5, pm, work Row 1 of Lace Stitch Patt to last 5 sts, pm, k5.

Row 2: P5, sl m, work Row 2 of Lace Stitch Patt to marker, sl m, p5.

Row 3: K5, sl m, work Row 3 of Lace Stitch Patt to marker, sl m, k5.

Row 4: P5, sl m, work Row 4 of Lace Stitch Patt to marker, sl m, p5.

Row 5: K5, sl m, work Row 5 of Lace Stitch Patt to marker, sl m, k5.

Row 6: P5, sl m, work Row 6 of Lace Stitch Patt to marker, sl m, p5.

Rep these 6 rows until piece measures approx 15¾"/40cm from cast-on edge, ending with a Row 3 or 6. Knit 6 rows, then BO all sts knitwise.

FINISHING

Weave in ends and block.

PREPARE BACKING

Cut a 17"/43cm square from underlay fabric.

Lay blocked lace piece, RS facing up, on top of underlay fabric (WS of lace piece will lie against RS of fabric). Carefully baste lace piece onto underlay, keeping lace taut.

Cut 2 rectangles from backing fabric, each 10"/25cm wide by 17"/43cm high. Using ½"/13mm hem, hem one long side of each rectangle (if backing fabric has nap or one-way design, lay out rectangles to make sure nap or one-way design is arranged accordingly).

Lay basted lace and underlay, RS facing up, on table. Place each rectangle RS facing down onto lace/underlay and pin. Carefully sew seam (using ½"/13mm seam allowance) around pillow. Turn cover right side out. Slide pillow form into opening formed by overlapping back rectangles.

Malbec Infinity Scarf

DESIGNER: Carol J. Sulcoski SKILL LEVEL: Easy

The contrast between light-as-air lace weight and plump bulky weight yarn creates an oddly pleasing asymmetry. This is a very quick knitting project that uses a relatively small amount of yarn, so splurge on some decadent handpaints or luxury fibers.

FINISHED MEASUREMENTS
Circumference 44"/112cm

Height 6¾"/17cm

MATERIALS AND TOOLS
Cephalopod Yarns Nautilace (40% baby camel/60% silk; 2oz/57g = 400yd/366m): (A), 1 skein, color Featherfin Squeaker #C19—approx 200yd/190m of lace weight yarn (0)

Koigu Bulky (100% merino; 3.5oz/100g = 93yd/85m); (B), 1 skein, color B20—approx 40yd/37m of bulky weight yarn (5)

Knitting needles: 9mm (size 13 U.S.) 24"/60cm or 32"/80cm circular needle or size to obtain gauge

Stitch marker

Tapestry needle

GAUGE
10 sts/16 rnds = 4"/10cm using A worked on 9mm (size 13 U.S.) needle in St st

Always take time to check your gauge.

INSTRUCTIONS

Note: Carry the yarn not in use up the back, twisting to avoid holes.

With A, CO 110 sts using knit cast-on, and join for working in the rnd, being careful not to twist. Place marker to show beg of rnd.

Rnd 1: Knit.

Rnd 2: Purl.

Rep Rnds 1 and 2 two more times, then work Rnd 1 only.

Switch to B, and knit 1 rnd.

Switch to A, and work Rnds 1 and 2 a total of 3 times (for 6 rnds).

Switch to B and knit 1 rnd.

Switch to A and purl 1 rnd.

Work Rnds 1 and 2 two more times, then work Rnd 1 only.

Switch to B, and knit 1 rnd.

Switch to A and work Rnds 1 and 2 three more times, then work Rnd 1 only.

BO all sts loosely.

FINISHING

Weave in ends carefully. Given how lightweight yarn A is and how loose the stitches are, you will not be able to completely conceal yarn B. Wear the join in the back if this bothers you.

Cosmos Cowl

DESIGNER: Carol J. Sulcoski SKILL LEVEL: Intermediate

I don't know why cables aren't used more in lace weight yarns. The airiness of the lightweight gauge and the filmy cloud of this gorgeous silk/mohair yarn make the single cable detail look fresh.

FINISHED MEASUREMENTS

Circumference 19"/48cm

Height 5"/13cm

MATERIALS AND TOOLS

Rowan Kidsilk Haze (70% superkid mohair/30% silk; 0.9oz/25g = 229yd/210m): 1 skein, color Splendour #00579—approx 150yd/137m of lace weight yarn (0)

Knitting needles: 3.75mm (size 5 U.S.) or size to obtain gauge

Waste yarn for provisional cast-on

2 stitch markers

Cable needle

Spare knitting needle (optional—if seaming with 3-needle bind-off)

Tapestry needle

GAUGE

24sts/28 rows = 4"/10cm in Cable Pattern worked on 3.75mm (size 5 U.S.), after blocking

Always take time to check your gauge.

INSTRUCTIONS

Notes:

1. Use stitch markers to set off the edging pattern from the actual cable.

2. Make sure you knit through the back loop on the RS only of the cable motif.

3. A sharper-tipped needle, such as an Addi Turbo Lace or Sock Rocket, may be helpful when knitting through the back loop.

4. Cowl is knit widthwise, back-and-forth, using provisional cast-on, then grafted together after blocking.

CO 31 sts using provisional cast-on.

Row 1 (RS): K3, p5, pm,[k1-tbl, p1] 7 times, k1-tbl, pm, p5, k3.

Row 2: K3, k5, sl m, [p1, k1] 7 times, p1, sl m, k5, k3.

Rows 3–14: Rep these 2 rows 6 more times.

Row 15: K3, p5, sl m, place next 7 sts on cn and hold at front of work, p1, [k1-tbl, p1] 3 times, k1-tbl, then [k1-tbl, p1] 3 times, k1-tbl from cn, sl m, p5, k3.

Row 16: Rep Row 2.

Rep these 16 rows until cowl measures approx 19"/48cm from first pattern row. Leave sts on needle and break off yarn, leaving a 24"/60cm tail.

FINISHING

Block flat, being careful not to drop live sts off needle. Remove provisional cast-on and place sts on spare needle. Join seam by either grafting two rows of live sts tog using Kitchener st (with RS facing out) or by using 3-needle bind-off with WS of work facing out. Weave in ends.

Scarlet Swag

DESIGNER: Barbara J. Brown SKILL LEVEL: Intermediate

If you're nervous about starting a big project or a little afraid of doing more detailed stitchwork for the first time in a lace weight yarn, this decorative swag is a great place to start. Give it a good blocking and it will look fantastic hanging from a mantel or staircase or adorning a crisp white tablecloth.

FINISHED MEASUREMENTS
Approx 80"/203cm by 3½"/9cm

MATERIALS AND TOOLS
Ancient Arts Fibres British BFL Lace (75% superwash merino/25% silk; 3.5oz/100g = 874yd/800m): 1 skein, color Syrah by Moonlight—approx 225yd/206m of lace weight yarn

Knitting needles: 4.5mm (size 7 U.S.) or size to obtain gauge

Tapestry needle

GAUGE
Each pattern repeat = 3½"/9cm x 2"/5cm after blocking, although gauge is less critical

Always take time to check your gauge.

INSTRUCTIONS

CO 17 sts.

Set-up row (WS): Sl 1 purlwise wyif, k to end of row.

Work 1 rep of Chart A.

Work 40 reps of Chart B, or until piece is desired length.

Work 1 rep of Chart A, then BO all sts.

FINISHING

Weave in ends and block.

Chart A

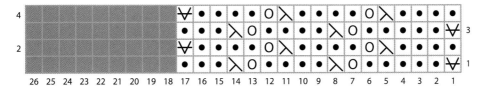

Chart B

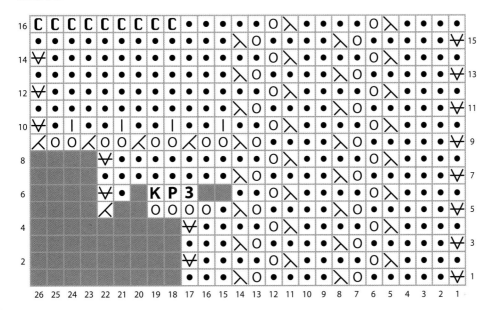

Key

•	**Knit** Knit on RS and WS (garter stitch).	▨	**No Stitch** Placeholder—No stitch made
∀	**Slip 1 purlwise** Insert tip of right needle into stitch as if to purl. Slip stitch off of left needle and onto right needle.	⊼	**K2tog** Knit 2 stitches together as 1 stitch
⋋	**SSK** Slip 2 stitches as if to knit. Insert LH needle into front of these 2 stitches and knit together.	I	**Purl** Purl Stitch
		C	**Cast off** Cast off stitch
O	**Yarn over** With yarn in front, bring yarn over top of Rneedle from front to back, creating 1 new stitch.	K P 3	**KP3** *K1, p1* 3 times into the 4 yo's of the previous row. Drop the forth YO. 6 stitches remain on needle.

Petite Odette Beaded Evening Bag

DESIGNER: Franklin Habit SKILL LEVEL: Experienced

Lush silk-blend lace weight yarn is both thin and strong—and thus perfect for holding beads. Use a thin crochet hook to place beads without prestringing them. The result is the perfect blend of vintage and modern. You'll want to carry this evening bag mornings and afternoons, too!

FINISHED MEASUREMENTS
Width 4"/10cm

Height 5"/12.5cm

MATERIALS AND TOOLS
Malabrigo Baby Silkpaca Lace (70% baby alpaca/30% silk; 1.75oz/50g= 420yd/384m): (A), 1 skein, color Indiecita #416—approx 120yd/110m of lace weight yarn 🄿

Knitting needles: Two 2.75mm (size 2 U.S.) 16"/40cm circular needles or size to obtain gauge

Toho Premium Japanese 6/0 "E" Silver-Lined Glass Beads: 4 tubes (9g/0.31oz) color 1952-48 High Metallic Purple, 3 tubes (9g/0.31oz) color 1952-16 Earl Grey

Coordinating lining fabric sufficient for finished size of bag (for measurements, see Instructions); sample uses less than ¼yd/0.25m purple polyester satin

Cotton or silk thread to match yarn

1.1mm (size 11 U.S.) steel crochet hook (for applying beads)

Locking ring stitch marker or safety pin

Tapestry needle

Sewing needle

Scissors for cutting thread and fabric

Silk, straight, or dressmaker's pins

Tailor's chalk

12"/30cm ruler

T-pin

GAUGE
34sts/48 rows = 4"/10cm in St st worked in rnds

Always take time to check your gauge.

SPECIAL ABBREVIATIONS
Yo2 – Double yarn over (yarn over right needle twice).

INSTRUCTIONS

Notes: To apply a bead when working charts, work as follows:

Place a bead on crochet hook. Slip next st from left-hand needle onto crochet hook; pull st through bead and place st on right-hand needle. On next round, work beaded stitch as usual.

With both circular needles, use Judy's Magic Cast-On to CO 68 sts (34 sts on each needle).

Rnd 1: Knit, placing marker into first st of needle 1 to mark it as beg of rnd.

Rnd 2: On first needle, k1, m1, k to last st, m1, k1—36 sts. Rep for second needle—72 sts total.

Work even in St st (k every rnd) until bag measures ¾"/2cm from CO.

Work Chart A across each needle.

Work even in St st for 5 rnds.

Work Chart B across each needle.

Eyelet rnd: [K1, k2tog, yo2, ssk] 6 times to last st of needle 1, k1. Rep for needle 2.

Next rnd: [K2, k first wrap, p second wrap, k1] 6 times to last st of needle 1, k1. Rep for needle 2.

Work Chart C across each needle.

BO in purl.

Break working yarn, leaving 6"/15cm tail.

FINISHING

Weave in all ends on WS.

LINING

Turn bag inside out and lay flat on work surface.

Measure width along bottom edge.

Measure length from bottom edge to just below eyelets.

Cut rectangle of lining fabric that measures:

- Length measurement x 2, plus 1"/2.5cm, by
- Width measurement plus 1"/2.5cm.

Fold lining in half with RS together and pin.

With tailor's chalk, mark seamlines ½"/13mm from each long selvage. Sew from bottom to ½"/13mm from top.

Turn lining RS out and slip inside-out bag into it. Align right and left sides of bag with right and left seams.

Turn top ½"/13mm of lining selvage toward bag and pin just below eyelets. (You may find it easier to do this one side at a time.)

Sew lining to bag.

When sewing is complete, turn bag RS out.

Strap:

Using ruler, measure and cut fifteen 48"/122cm lengths of yarn.

Separate the lengths into 3 bundles of 5 strands each.

Tie the 3 bundles together at one end with a length of scrap yarn. Use the T-pin to attach this end to a blocking mat, sofa cushion, or other flat surface.

Braid the 3 bundles together neatly and evenly.

When the end of the braid is reached, tie it together.

Run the braid through the eyelets of the bag.

Align the tips of the braid. Run a 24"/60cm length of yarn through both ends of the braid, about 2½"/6cm from the tips. Tie firmly with a secure knot. Wrap the knot generously with the loose ends of the yarn and bury the loose ends securely in the wraps. Unbraid the tips, fluff into a tassel, and trim tassel ends neatly.

Chart A

Key

- ⬛ purple bead
- ⬛ gray bead
- ⬜ plain stitch (knit)

Chart B

Chart C

Eden Scarf

DESIGNER: Carol J. Sulcoski SKILL LEVEL: Easy

Make the most of a lace weight mohair blend by creating airy poufs of fabric, cinched into place by a glorious handpainted fingering weight yarn. This project is dramatic and striking but super easy to knit, and would make a great gift.

FINISHED MEASUREMENTS

Width 5"/13cm (measuring seed stitch bands)

Length 50"/127cm

MATERIALS AND TOOLS

Koigu Painter's Palette Premium Merino (100% merino wool; 1.75oz/50g=170yd/160m): (A), 1 skein, color Green/Blue/Gold Multi #3611X—approx 150yd/137m of fingering weight yarn (1)

Classic Elite Yarns Pirouette (67% kid mohair/25% bamboo viscose/8% nylon; 0.9oz/25g=246yd/225m): (B) 2 skeins, color Chartreuse #4035—approx 400yd/366m of lace weight yarn (0)

Knitting needles: 3.25mm (size 3 U.S.) or size to obtain gauge

4.5mm (size 7 U.S.) or four sizes larger than previous needle

Tapestry needle

GAUGE

24 sts/40 rows = 4"/10cm using (A) worked on 3.25mm (size 3 U.S.) needles in Seed st

20 sts/28 rows = 4"/10cm using (B) worked on 4.5mm (size 7 U.S.) needles in St st

Always take time to check your gauge.

PATTERN STITCH

Seed Stitch (multiple of 2 sts + 1):

Row 1: K1, *p1, k1, rep from * to end.

Rep this row.

INSTRUCTIONS

With smaller needles and A, CO 25 sts.

Work in Seed St for 8 rows.

Next row (RS): Pick up B and holding it together with A, work 2 more rows of Seed St using both yarns.

Break off A.

Next row (RS): With B only, *k in first loop of A, then k a new st in first loop of B (creating 2 sts by knitting 1 in each loop of the double-stranded sts), rep from * to end—50 sts.

Next row (WS): Switch to larger needles and purl.

Cont using larger needle and B only, work in St st until scarf measures approx 6"/15cm from last row of Seed St; end with a WS row.

Next row: *K2tog, rep from * to end—25 sts.

Next row (WS): Switch to smaller needles and purl.

Join A again, and work 2 rows of Seed St double-stranded.

Break off B, and working with A only, work 8 rows of Seed St.

Rep portion between brackets 6 more times.

Using A and smaller needles, BO all sts.

FINISHING

Weave in ends and lightly steam block, being careful not to crush mohair sections.

Two SKEIN PROJECTS

Garnet Valley Hat

DESIGNER: Carol J. Sulcoski SKILL LEVEL: Easy

A lightweight hat is less likely to result in the dreaded "hat hair," and this snappy number features slip stitches that mimic the usually hidden floats that come with stranded knitting. The yarn is doubled for the ribbed section only, giving a closer, sturdier fit at the brim.

FINISHED MEASUREMENTS
Circumference 20"/51cm

MATERIALS AND TOOLS
Three Fates Yarns Lechesis Merino Laceweight (100% superwash merino; 4 oz/150g = 968yd/885m): (MC), 1 skein, color Center Stage—approx 250yd/229m of lace weight yarn (0)

Black Bunny Fibers Merino-Silk Laceweight(70% merino/30% silk; 1.75oz/50g = 430yd/393m): (CC), small amount, color Natural—approx 50yd/46m of lace weight yarn (0)

Knitting needles: 3.25mm (size 3 U.S.) 16"/40cm circular needle or size to obtain gauge

Double-pointed needles in same size as above

Stitch markers

Tapestry needle

GAUGE
28 sts/40rnds = 4"/10cm using single strand of MC worked on 3.25mm (size 3 U.S.) needles

Always take time to check your gauge.

SPECIAL ABBREVIATION
S2kp –Slip next 2 sts tog knitwise; knit next st; pass 2 slipped sts over knit st—2 stsdec.

PATTERN STITCHES

Ribbing Pattern (multiple of 4 sts):

Rnd 1: *K2, p2, rep from * to end.

Rep this rnd.

Slip Stitch Stripe Sequence (multiple of 6 sts):

Begin by setting up CC at beg of rnd as if adding a color for stranded knitting.

Rnd 1: K1 with MC, *bring CC to front of work, p1 in CC, leave CC at front of work, k2 in MC, p1 in CC, take CC to back of work, k2 in MC, rep from * to last 5 sts, bring CC to front of work, p1 in CC, leave CC at front of work, k2 in MC, p1 in CC, take CC to back of work, k1 in MC.

Rnds 2 and 3: Using MC, knit.

Rnd 4: Rep Rnd 1.

Rnds 5–9: Using MC, knit.

INSTRUCTIONS

Edging:

Using 2 strands of MC held tog, CO 120 sts. Join for knitting in the rnd, being careful not to twist. Place marker to show beg of rnd.

Work Ribbing Patt until hat measures 1¼"/3cm from beg.

Incrnd: Break off one strand of MC, using remaining single strand as working yarn, and *k5, treating double strands as a single st; k1 in one strand of next st, k1 in remaining strand of same st, rep from * to end—140 sts.

Body of Hat:

K every rnd until hat measures 2"/5cm from beg.

K 1 rnd, dec 2 sts evenly around—138 sts.

Work Slip Stitch Stripe Sequence a total of 5 times. Break off CC.

Shape Crown:

K 1 rnd, dec 3 sts evenly around—135 sts.

Dec rnd: K12, *s2kp, k24, rep from * to last 15 sts, s2kp, k to end—125 sts.

Next rnd: Knit.

Dec rnd: K11, *s2kp, k22, rep from * to last 14 sts, s2kp, k to end—115 sts.

Next rnd: Knit.

Dec rnd: K10, *s2kp, k20, rep from * to last 13 sts, s2kp, k to end—105 sts.

Next rnd: Knit.

Cont in this manner until all sts between decreases are used up—5 sts rem.

Break off yarn and fasten off these sts.

FINISHING

Weave in ends and block as desired.

Turquoise Trail Shawl

DESIGNER: Erika Flory SKILL LEVEL: Easy

Easy openwork stitches and simple Stockinette stitch paired with a stunning yarn create a light breath of a shawl. Worked from the tip to the base, this triangular piece is a great introduction to the basic stitches used in lace knitting.

FINISHED MEASUREMENTS

Wingspan 66"/168cm

Center back 31"/79cm

MATERIALS AND TOOLS

Black Bunny Fibers Heavenly Lace (70% baby alpaca/20% silk/10% cashmere; 3.5oz/100g = 1300yd/1189m): 1 skein, color Jive Turquoise—approx 875yd/800m of lace weight yarn (0)

Knitting needles: 3.5mm (size 4 U.S.) 26"/66cm circular needle or size to obtain gauge

Stitch marker

Tapestry needle

GAUGE

18 sts/25 rows = 4"/10cm in St st, after blocking

Always take time to check your gauge.

SPECIAL ABBREVIATION

Kfb (knit into front and back) – Knit into the front and back of the next stitch—inc 1 st.

INSTRUCTIONS

CO 2 sts.

Set-up:

Row 1 (RS): K1, kfb—3 sts.

Row 2: Knit.

Row 3: K1, kfb, k to end—4 sts.

Row 4: Knit.

Rep Rows 3 and 4 until there are 9 sts on needle.

Shawl Body:

Row 1 (RS): K1, kfb, pm, k2tog, (yo) twice, ssk, k3—10 sts.

Row 2: K3, k1, (k1, p1) in double yo, k1, sl marker, k3.

Row 3: K1, kfb, k to marker, sl marker, k2tog, (yo) twice, ssk, k3—11 sts.

Row 4: K4, (k1, p1) in double yo, k1, sl marker, p to last 3 sts, k3.

Rep Rows 3 and 4 until there are 34 sts on needle, removing marker on last row as you come to it.

Next Section:

Row 1 (RS): K1, kfb, k18, pm, *k2tog, (yo) twice, ssk, k3; rep from * to end of row—35 sts.

Row 2: K4, (k1, p1) in double yo, k1, p3, k1, (k1, p1) in double yo, k1, sl marker, p to last 3 sts, k3.

Row 3: K1, kfb, k to marker, sl marker, *k2tog, (yo) twice, ssk, k3; rep from * to end of row—36 sts.

Row 4: K4, (k1, p1) in double yo, k1, p3, k1, (k1, p1) in double yo, k1, sl marker, p to last 3 sts, k3.

Rep Rows 3 and 4 until there are 59 sts on needle, removing marker on last row as you come to it.

Next Section:

Row 1 (RS): K1, kfb, k36, pm, *k2tog, (yo) twice, ssk, k3; rep from * to end of row—60 sts.

Row 2: K3, *k1, (k1, p1) in double yo, k1, p3; rep from * 2 more times, p to last 3 sts, slipping marker as you come to it, k3.

Row 3: K1, kfb, k to marker, sl marker, *k2tog, (yo) twice, ssk, k3; rep from * to end of row—61 sts.

Row 4: K3, *k1, (k1, p1) in double yo, k1, p3; rep from * 2 more times, p to last 3 sts, slipping marker as you come to it, k3.

Rep Rows 3 and 4 until there are 84 sts on needle, removing marker on last row as you come to it.

Next Section:

Row 1 (RS): K1, kfb, k54, pm, *k2tog, (yo) twice, ssk, k3; rep from * to end of row—85 sts.

Row 2: K3, *k1, (k1, p1) in double yo, k1, p3; rep from * 3 more times, p to last 3 sts, slipping marker as you come to it, k3.

Row 3: K1, kfb, k to marker, sl marker, *k2tog, (yo) twice, ssk, k3; rep from * to end of row—86 sts.

Row 4: K3, *k1, (k1, p1) in double yo, k1, p3; rep from * 3 more times, p to last 3 sts, slipping marker as you come to it, k3.

Rep Rows 3 and 4 until there are 109 sts on needle, removing marker on last row as you come to it.

Next Section:

Row 1 (RS): K1, kfb, k72, pm, *k2tog, (yo) twice, ssk, k3; rep from * to end of row—110 sts.

Row 2: K3, *k1, (k1, p1) in double yo, k1, p3; rep from * 4 more times, p to last 3 sts, slipping marker as you come to it, k3.

Row 3: K1, kfb, k to marker, sl marker, *k2tog, (yo) twice, ssk, k3; rep from * to end of row—111 sts.

Row 4: K3, *k1, (k1, p1) in double yo, k1, p3; rep from * 4 more times, p to last 3 sts, slipping marker as you come to it, k3.

Rep Rows 3 and 4 until there are 134 sts on needle, removing marker on last row as you come to it.

Openwork Edging:

Row 1 (RS): K1, kfb, pm, k1, *yo, k2tog; rep from * to last 3 sts, k3—135 sts.

Row 2: K3, p to last 3 sts, sl marker, k3.

Row 3: K1, kfb, k1, sl marker, *ssk, yo; rep from * to last 4 sts, k4—136 sts.

Row 4: K3, p to marker, sl marker, p1, k3.

Row 5: K1, kfb, k to marker, sl marker, k1, *yo, k2tog; rep from * to last 3 sts, k3—137 sts.

Row 6: K3, p to marker, sl marker, p2, k3.

Row 7: K1, kfb, k to marker, sl marker, *ssk, yo; rep from * to last 4 sts, k4—138 sts.

Row 8: K3, p to marker, sl marker, p3, k3.

Row 9: K1, kfb, k to marker, sl marker, k1, *yo, k2tog; rep from * to last 3 sts, k3—139 sts.

Row 10: K3, p to marker, sl marker, p4, k3.

Row 11: K1, kfb, k to marker, sl marker, *ssk, yo; rep from * to last 4 sts, k4—140 sts.

Row 12: K3, p to marker, remove marker, p5, k3.

Work Rows 1–12 four more times for a total of 5 repeats—164 sts.

Knit 4 rows.

BO loosely.

FINISHING

Weave in ends. Block to finished measurements.

Elswyth Scarf

DESIGNER: Carol J. Sulcoski SKILL LEVEL: Intermediate

Pump up the drama by pairing two shades of lace weight, shown here in nature-inspired colors perhaps not traditionally associated with lace. Knit the edging first, and then pick up stitches along the long edge and work up to finish.

FINISHED MEASUREMENTS

Width 8"/20cm, after blocking

Length 60"/152cm, after blocking

MATERIALS AND TOOLS

Black Bunny Fibers Merino-Silk Laceweight (70% merino/30% silk; 1.75oz/50g = 430yd/393m): (A), 1 skein, color Evergreen; (B), 1 skein, color Bark—approx 250yd/229m of lace weight yarn (0) in A and approx 400yd/366m of lace weight yarn in B (0)

Knitting needles: 4mm (size 6 U.S.) 32"/80cm circular needle or size to obtain gauge

GAUGE

20 sts/28 rows = 4½"/10cm worked on size 4mm (size 6 U.S.) needles, after blocking

Always take time to check your gauge.

SPECIAL ABBREVIATION

Skp – Sl 1 st, k 1 st, pass slipped st over–dec 1 st.

PATTERN STITCHES

Edging Pattern (beg over 13 sts):

Row 1: K7, yo, skp, yo, k4.

Row 2 (WS) and all odd-numbered rows: K2, p to last 2 sts, k2.

Row 3: K6, [yo, skp] twice, yo, k4.

Row 5: K5, [yo, skp] 3 times, yo, k4.

Row 7: K4, [yo, skp] 4 times, yo, k4.

Row 9: K3, [yo, skp] 5 times, yo, k4.

Row 11: K4, [yo, skp] 5 times, k2tog, k2.

Row 13: K5, [yo, skp] 4 times, k2tog, k2.

Row 15: K6, [yo, skp] 3 times, k2tog, k2.

Row 17: K7, [yo, skp] twice, k2tog, k2.

Row 19: K8, yo, skp, k2tog, k2.

Row 20: K2, p to last 2 sts, k2.

Eyelet Pattern (multiple of 8 sts + 7):

Row 1 (RS): Knit.

Row 2 and all even-numbered rows: K4, p to last 4 sts, k4.

Row 3: K7, *yo, skp, k6, rep from * to end.

Row 5: K5, *k2tog, yo, k1, yo, skp, k3, rep from * to last 2 sts, k2.

Row 7: Rep Row 3.

Row 9: Knit.

Row 11: K11, *yo, skp, k6, rep from * to last 4 sts, k4.

Row 13: K9, *k2tog, yo, k1, yo, skp, k3, rep from * to last 6 sts, k6.

Row 15: Rep Row 11.

Row 16: K4, p to last 4 sts, k4.

INSTRUCTIONS

Edging:

Using A, CO 13 sts.

Set-up row (WS): K2, p to last 2 sts, k2.

Work Edging Patt until piece measures approx 60"/152cm long when gently stretched. BO all sts.

Switch to B, and with RS facing, pick up 303 sts across straight long edge of edging piece.

Set-up row (WS): K4, p to last 4 sts, k4.

Work Eyelet Patt for approx 5"/13cm.

K 8 rows, then BO all sts loosely.

FINISHING

Weave in all ends, then block.

Square in the Round Poncho

DESIGNER: Robyn M. Schrager SKILL LEVEL: *Easy*

This raglan-shaped poncho is knit top down in-the-round, while the pinstripes create the illusion of being in-the-square. Wear it with the widest part in front, or rotated 90 degrees for an angular look. So frothy it seems to float, so sheer the warmth is unexpected, and shining with a subdued sparkle, this garment can be worn year-round.

FINISHED MEASUREMENTS

Neck opening 14"/36cm

Length (at lower edge) 43"/109cm

Length 14"/36cm

MATERIAL AND TOOLS

Schulana Kid-Seta (70% kid mohair/30% silk; 0.88oz/25g = 231yd/211m): (A), 2 skeins, color Deep Teal #16—approx 375yd/343m of lace weight yarn

Schulana Kid-Seta Lux (71% super kid mohair/20% silk/9% lurex; 0.88oz/25g = 229yd/209m): (B), 1 skein, color Cream #210—approx 185yd/168m of lace weight yarn

Knitting needles: 5mm (size 8 U.S.) 24"/60cm circular needle (you may choose to switch to 32"/80cm and 40"/100cm needles as the garment grows wider) or size to obtain gauge

Stitch markers

Tapestry needle

GAUGE

15 sts/20 rows = 4"/10cm in St st

Always take time to check your gauge.

INSTRUCTIONS

Note: Cast-on edge will become garment neckline.

With A, CO 100 sts.

Set-Up Row 1: With A, knit, then join for working in the rnd, being careful not to twist.

Set-Up Rnd 2: K13, pm, k1, pm, k35, pm, k1, pm, k13, pm, k1, pm, k35, pm, k1, pm.

Set-Up Rnds 3 and 4: Knit.

Set-Up Rnds 5 and 6: With B, knit.

Set-Up Rnds 7 and 8: With A, knit.

Rnd 1 (Inc rnd): With A, [yo, knit to marker, yo, sl marker, k1, sl marker] 3 times, yo, knit to next marker, yo, sl marker, k1, sl marker—108 sts.

Rnd 2: Knit.

Rep last 2 rnds 3 times—132 sts.

With B, rep Rnd 1 (Inc rnd) and Rnd 2—140 sts.

With A, rep Rnds 1 and 2—148 sts.

Rep last 4 rnds, alternating 2 rnds worked with A and 2 rnds worked with B, until you have completed 3 color B pinstripes (not including the pinstripe worked in the Set-Up Rnds).

With A, rep Rnds 1 and 2 until poncho measures 10"/25cm. (If you want your poncho to be longer than the sample, this is the time to add more rounds.)

With B, rep Rnds 1 and 2.

With A, rep Rnds 1 and 2.

Rep last 4 rnds until you have completed 2 color B pinstripes. Remove markers when working next rnd.

Stop increasing, but continue in pinstripe pattern until you have a total of 5 color B pinstripes.

Cut B.

Knit with A for 1"/2.5cm.

BO loosely.

FINISHING

Weave in ends. Steam lightly and gently shake to fluff the mohair.

Schematic

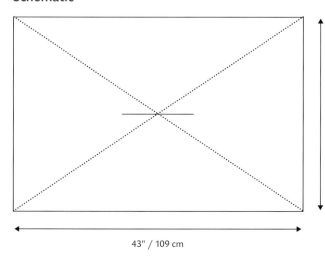

28" / 71 cm

43" / 109 cm

Blue River Cowl

DESIGNER: Elizabeth Morrison SKILL LEVEL: Easy

Have a little bit of lace yarn left over from a bigger project? This cowl lets you make the most of it by pairing it with fingering weight yarn in a slipstitch pattern. Although the needles are small, the work goes quickly. This is the kind of project you can take along and work on with minimal attention.

FINISHED MEASUREMENTS
Circumference 28"/71cm

Height 9"/23cm

MATERIALS AND TOOLS
Black Bunny Fibers Suri Sparkle Lace (80% suri alpaca/15% merino/5% stellina; 4.4oz/125g = 1090yd/978m): (A), 1 ball, color Green Sleeves—approx 270yd/247m of lace weight yarn (0)

Triskelion Yarn and Fibre Gofannnon 4 ply (100% baby alpaca; 3.5oz/100g = 437yd/400m): (B), 1 ball, color Barinthus—approx 220yd/201m of fingering yarn (1)

Knitting needles: 2.75 mm (size 2 U.S.) 24"/40cm circular needle or size to obtain gauge

2.75 mm (size 2 U.S.)set of double-pointed needles

1 stitch marker

Tapestry needle

2 buttons, 1⅛"/28mm

GAUGE
27 sts/26 rows = 4"/10cm in pattern stitch, after blocking

Always take time to check your gauge.

INSTRUCTIONS

Note: Slip stitches purlwise with yarn in back (on wrong side of fabric).

With circular needle and B, using a fairly stretchy cast-on, CO 192 sts. Join to work in rounds. Place marker at end of round.

Border:

Purl 1 rnd.

Knit 1 rnd.

Purl 1 rnd.

Main Section:

Join A.

Rnd 1: Switch to A, knit 1 rnd.

Rnd 2: Purl 1 rnd.

Rnd 3: Switch to B, k1, *sl 1, k3; rep from * to last 3sts, sl 1, k2.

Rnd 4: P1, *sl 1, p3; rep from * to last 3 sts, sl 1, p2.

Rnds 5 and 6: Switch to A, rep Rnds 1 and 2.

Rnd 7: Switch to B, *k3, sl 1; rep from * around.

Rnd 8: *P3, sl 1; rep from * around.

Rep these 8 rnds until work measures about 8"/20cm unstretched from beg. End after a Row 2 or a Row 6. Switch to B for upper edging. Break A.

Upper Edging:

With B, knit 1 rnd.

Purl 1 rnd.

Knit 1 rnd.

BO with reasonably-stretchy bind-off.

FINISHING

I-cord button loops (make 2):

With double-pointed needles and B, CO 4 sts. Work I-cord for 3½"/9cm. BO.

Note: Leave long enough tail on each end for sewing to main cowl.

Measure 2"/5cm down from top and 2"/5cm up from bottom of cowl, about 5"/13cm to the right of center front. Attach each I-cord to main cowl by darning into a loop shape and sewing to main cowl (see schematic for placement).

Place buttons to correspond to button loops, 2"/5cm from top and bottom edges, 5"/13cm to left of center front. Sew in place. Note: Thin nylon yarn as sold for reinforcing socks works well for this.

Weave in ends. Wet block piece, tugging vertically to enhance stitch pattern.

Schematic

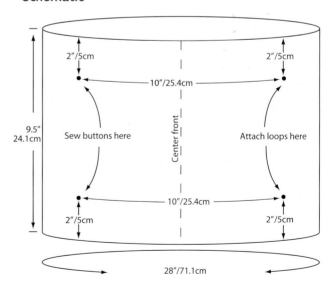

Blue Diamond Lace Scarf

DESIGNER: Marly Bird SKILL LEVEL: Intermediate

Combine a luscious blend of angora and viscose, a rich saturated color, and a geometric eyelet pattern and you get a beautiful example of modern lace! Versatile, luxurious, and just plain gorgeous.

FINISHED MEASUREMENTS

Width 11"/28cm

Length 84"/213cm

MATERIALS AND TOOLS

Bijou Basin Ranch Seraphim (95% angora/5% viscose; 1.75 oz/50g = 435yd/398m); 2 skeins, color Eggplant—approx 870yd/796m of lace weight yarn

Knitting needles: 5mm (size 8 U.S.) or size to obtain gauge

Tapestry needle

Stitch holder

GAUGE

One full repeat of Lace Diamond Pattern is 2½"/6cm wide and just under 5"/13cm tall, after blocking

Always take time to check your gauge.

INSTRUCTIONS

Notes: Scarf is worked in two halves. Each half is worked from the ripple edging toward the center.

Halves are grafted together at center.

Knit the first 4 sts of every row.

When you reach the last 4 sts of each row, k3 sts, then slip the last st with yarn in front (wyif).

First Half:

CO 57 sts.

Set-up row: K4, p to last 4 sts, k3, sl 1 wyif.

Edging:

Next 28 rows: K4, beg with Row 1 work the Ripple Chart, repeating the portion outlined in red 3 times, k3, sl 1 wyif.

Transition:

Next 10 rows: K4, beg with Row 1 work the Transition Chart, repeating the portion outlined in red 3 times, k3, sl 1 wyif.

Body:

Next 24 rows: K4, beg with Row 1 work the Diamond Lace Chart, repeating the portion outlined in red 3 times, k3, sl 1 wyif.

Rep last 24 rows until chart has been worked a total of 7 times.

Next 13 rows: K4, beg with Row 1 and ending with Row 13 work Diamond Lace Chart, repeating the portion outlined in red 3 times, k3, sl 1 wyif.

Place sts on holder. Cut yarn.

Second Half:

Work same as First Half until Diamond Lace Chart has been worked a total of 7 times.

Next 15 rows: K4, beg with Row 1 and ending with Row 15 work Diamond Lace Chart, repeating the portion outlined in red 3 times, k3, sl 1 wyif.

Cut yarn, leaving a long enough tail to graft the stitches of the two halves together.

FINISHING

Graft the two halves of the scarf together using Kitchener st.

Weave in ends and block scarf to final measurements.

Transition Chart

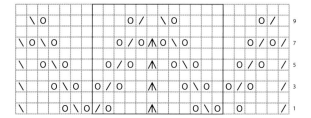

Ripple Chart

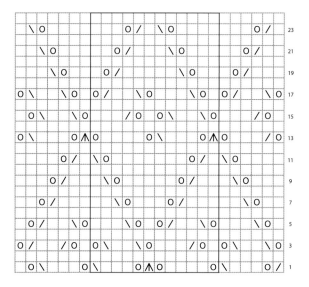

Diamond Lace Chart

Key

Knit
Knit on RS, Purl on WS.

K2tog
Knit 2 stitches together as 1 stitch.

SSK
Slip 1 stitch as if to knit. Slip another stitch as if to knit. Insert LH needle into front of these 2 stitches and knit them together.

S2psso
Slip 2 together as if to knit, K1, pass 2 stitches over.

Yarn over
With yarn in front, bring yarn over top of needle from front to back, creating 1 new stitch.

Récherché Vest and Scarf

DESIGNER: Véronik Avery SKILL LEVEL: Intermediate

It's hard to believe that only one or two skeins of yarn are needed to create this beautiful openwork vest. And it's also hard to believe that the exquisitely soft and downy yarn is made from bison down—yes, bison, as in buffalo. The natural color of this luxurious fiber is complemented gloriously by this mesh-and-lace design.

SIZES
XS (S, M, L, 1X, 2X, 3X)

FINISHED MEASUREMENTS

Vest

Bust 31 (34, 37, 40, 43, 46, 49)"/79 (86, 94, 102, 109, 117, 124)cm

Length 24 (24¾, 25½, 26¼, 27, 28, 28¾)"/61 (63, 65, 67, 69, 71, 73)cm

Scarf

Width 15¼"/39cm

Length 58"/147cm

MATERIALS AND TOOLS

Vest

The Buffalo Wool Co. Heaven (100% bison down; 1.75oz/50g = 400yd/366m): 1 (1, 1, 2, 2, 2, 2) skeins, color Natural Brown—approx 303 (336, 371, 413, 447, 500, 540)yd/277 (307, 339, 378, 409, 457, 494)m of lace weight yarn (0)

Scarf

The Buffalo Wool Co. Heaven (100% bison down; 1.75oz/50g = 400yd/366m): 1 skein, color Natural Brown—approx 320yd/293m of lace weight yarn (0)

Knitting needles: 4mm (size 6 U.S.) or size to obtain gauge

Stitch markers

Stitch holders

Waste yarn

Blocking wires (optional)

GAUGE

17 sts/32 rows = 4"/10cm over Lace Panel Chart before blocking

16 sts/28 rows = 4"/10cm over Lace Panel Chart after blocking

Always take time to check your gauge.

Work in Garter st (k 1 rnd, p 1 rnd) for 6 rnds.

Set-up rnd: *K1, work Round 1 of Background Lace Chart over next 30 (33, 36, 39, 42, 45, 48) sts, PM, work Round 1 of Lace Panel Chart over next 25 sts, PM, work Round 1 of Background Lace Chart over next 30 (33, 36, 39, 42, 45, 48) sts; PM for side; rep from * once more.

Work 3 rnds in established patt.

Body Decrease rnd: *Work to 2 sts before next marker, work left-slanting decrease, sl marker, work across Lace Panel in established patt, sl marker, work right-slanting decrease, work to side marker, sl marker; rep from * once more—168 (180, 192, 204, 216, 228, 240) sts.

Rep Body Decrease rnd every 12th rnd 8 times more while working Lace Panel decreases as indicated on chart—124 (136, 148, 160, 172, 184, 196) sts rem.

Work even until body measures 15¾ (16, 16¼, 16 ²/₄, 16 ¾, 17¼, 17 ²/₄)"/40 (41, 41, 42, 43, 44, 44)cm, ending after an odd-numbered rnd.

Divide for Front and Back:

At this point, you should have 19 sts each in the front and back center Lace Panels, and 43 (49, 55, 61, 67, 73, 79) sts each in Background Lace between the Lace Panels (including the k1 at the center of each Background Lace section).

Prepare four 12"/30cm pieces of waste yarn. Using a tapestry needle, thread the pieces as if using a "lifeline" as follows:

1. Thread one piece through the 9th, 10th, and 11th st of each center Lace Panel (the center 3 sts of each panel).

2. Thread one piece through the center 3 sts of each Background Lace section (the 3 center sts include the st before the center k1, the center k1, and the st following the center k1).

Secure free ends of each piece. Do not remove stitches from needle. You will work into these stitches in the next row. You will also pick up these stitches again later to create the "twist" where backs and fronts meet.

Next row (RS): Remove beg of rnd marker, k2, turn.

Next row (WS): K3, p28 (31, 34, 37, 40, 43, 46), k3—34 (37, 40, 43, 46, 49, 52) Left Back sts.

INSTRUCTIONS

Notes: Vest is worked in rnds beginning at lower edge. Piece is divided at armholes and backs and fronts worked separately, in rows, to shoulders.

When shaping in Background Lace patt, work decreases as follows:

For left-slanting decreases:

- for stitches that would normally be knit in St st or when 2 sts remain between last repeat and marker, [ssk].

- for a full repeat [yo, k3tog, yo], substitute [yo, k3tog].

For right-slanting decreases:

- for stitches that would normally be knit in St st or when 2 sts remain between marker and first repeat, [k2tog].

- for a full repeat [yo, k3tog, yo], substitute [k3tog, yo].

Vest:

Beg at lower edge, CO 172 (184, 196, 208, 220, 232, 244), PM, and join for working in the rnd, being careful not to twist.

Left Back:

Work is now knit back and forth on Left Back. Place next 31 (34, 37, 40, 43, 46, 49) sts on waste yarn or holder for Right Back, next 31 (34, 37, 40, 43, 46, 49) sts on waste yarn for Right Front, next 28 (31, 34, 37, 40, 43, 46) sts on waste yarn for Left Front, then continue on 34 (37, 40, 43, 46, 49, 52) sts for Left Back.

Dec Row 1 (RS): K2, work left-slanting dec, work in patt to last 4 sts, work right-slanting dec, k3—32 (35, 38, 41, 44, 47, 50) sts rem.

Next row and all WS rows: Keeping first and last 3 sts in Garter st (k every row), work even in established patt.

Dec Row 2 (RS): K3, work in patt to last 4 sts, work right-slanting dec, k3—31 (34, 37, 40, 43, 46, 49) sts rem.

Rep Dec Rows 1 and 2 once more—28 (31, 34, 37, 40, 43, 46) sts.

Rep Dec Row 1 every 4th row 1 (4, 7, 7, 7, 10, 10) times more—26 (23, 20, 23, 26, 23, 26) sts.

Work even in established patt for 3 rows.

Last Dec Row: K2, work left-slanting dec, work in patt to end—25 (22, 19, 22, 25, 22, 25) sts.

Rep Last Dec Row every 4th row 7 (4, 1, 1, 4, 1, 1) time(s)—18 (18, 18, 21, 21, 21, 24) sts rem.

Work even until armhole measures 8¼ (8¾, 9¼, 9¾, 10¼, 10¾, 11¼)"/21 (22, 23, 25, 26, 27, 29)cm. Place all sts on holder.

Right Back:

With WS facing and tip of RH needle, carefully slip the 3 center back sts from the "lifeline" to the needle so that they can be worked again, then replace 31 (34, 37, 40, 43, 46, 49) Right Back sts to needle—34 (37, 40, 43, 46, 49, 52) Right Back sts. Join yarn at center back and beg with WS row.

Next row (WS): K3, p28 (31, 34, 37, 40, 43, 46), k3.

Dec Row 1 (RS): K3, work left-slanting dec, work in patt to last 3 sts, work right-slanting dec, k2—32 (35, 38, 41, 44, 47, 50) sts rem.

Next row and all WS rows: Keeping first and last 3 sts in Garter st, work even in established patt.

Dec Row 2: K3, work left-slanting dec, work in patt to last 3 sts, k3—31 (34, 37, 40, 43, 46, 49) sts rem.

Repeat Dec Rows 1 and 2 once more—28 (31, 34, 37, 40, 43, 46) sts.

Rep Dec Row 1 on every 4th row 1 (4, 7, 7, 7, 10, 10) times more—26 (23, 20, 23, 26, 23, 26) sts.

Work even in established patt for 3 rows.

Last Dec Row: K3, work in patt to last 4 sts, work right-slanting dec, k2—25 (22, 19, 22, 25, 22, 25) sts.

Rep Last Dec Row every 4th row 7 (4, 1, 1, 4, 1, 1) time(s)—18 (18, 18, 21, 21, 21, 24) sts rem.

Work even until armhole measures 8¼ (8¾, 9 ¼, 9¾, 10¼, 10¾, 11¼)"/21 (22, 23, 25, 26, 27, 29)cm. Place all sts on holder.

Right Front:

With WS facing and tip of RH needle, carefully slip the 3 center side sts from the "lifeline" to the needle, then replace 31 (34, 37, 40, 43, 46, 49) Right Front sts to needle—34 (37, 40, 43, 46, 49, 52) Right Front sts. Join yarn at side seam and beg with WS row. Cont as for Left Back.

Left Front:

With WS facing and tip of RH needle, carefully slip the 3 center front sts from the "lifeline" to the needle, replace 28 (31, 34, 37, 40, 43, 46) Left Front sts, then

slip the 3 center side sts from the rem "lifeline" to the needle—34 (37, 40, 43, 46, 49, 52) Left Front sts. Join yarn at center Front and beg with WS row. Cont as for Right Back.

FINISHING

With WS facing, and using 3-needle bind-off method, join straps together.

Weave in loose ends. Block to finished measurements.

Scarf:

Half (make 2):

CO 6 sts using a provisional method.

Knit 1 WS row.

Shape Point:

Row 1 (RS): K3, yo, k3—7 sts.

Row 2 and all WS rows: K3, p to last 3 sts, k3.

Row 3: K3, yo, k to last 3 sts, yo, k3—9 sts.

Repeat Rows 2 and 3 until there are 31 sts on needles, then work Row 2 once more.

Next row (RS): K3, yo, work Row 1 of Lace Panel Chart over next 25 sts, yo, k3—33 sts.

Cont increasing on each side of Lace Panel every RS row until there are 61 sts on needles, working new sts in Background Lace Chart.

Work even until scarf measures approximately 29"/74cm, after completing a WS row.

Join Ends:

With WS held tog, BO the two ends tog as follows: *With yarn between needles, slip first st on front needle knitwise, then purl first st on back needle*; psso; rep from * to *, then pass the first 2 sts on right needle over the purled st. Cont in this manner, passing the first 2 sts over the purled st, until 31 sts have been bound off. Turn pieces around to BO from opposite edge toward the center, using 2nd tail and keeping WS together. BO rem 30 sts, plus the single st at center in the same manner as before. Cut yarn and fasten off last st.

FINISHING

Weave in loose ends. Block to finished measurements.

Vest Schematic

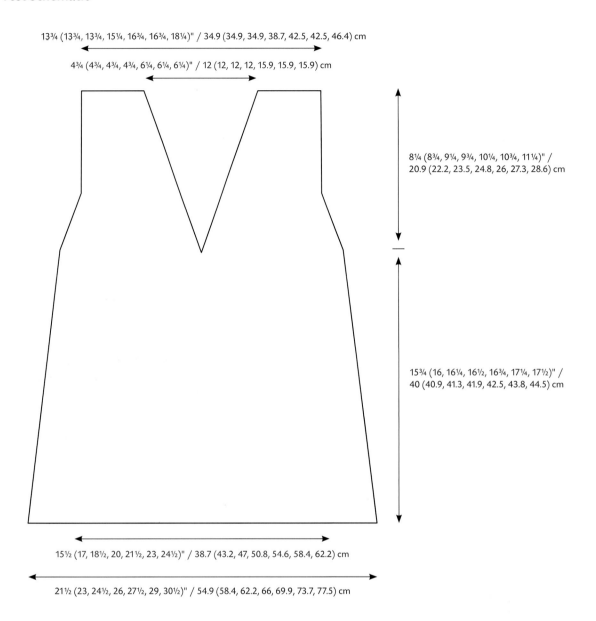

13¾ (13¾, 13¾, 15¼, 16¾, 16¾, 18¼)" / 34.9 (34.9, 34.9, 38.7, 42.5, 42.5, 46.4) cm

4¾ (4¾, 4¾, 4¾, 6¼, 6¼, 6¼)" / 12 (12, 12, 12, 15.9, 15.9, 15.9) cm

8¼ (8¾, 9¼, 9¾, 10¼, 10¾, 11¼)" / 20.9 (22.2, 23.5, 24.8, 26, 27.3, 28.6) cm

15¾ (16, 16¼, 16½, 16¾, 17¼, 17½)" / 40 (40.9, 41.3, 41.9, 42.5, 43.8, 44.5) cm

15½ (17, 18½, 20, 21½, 23, 24½)" / 38.7 (43.2, 47, 50.8, 54.6, 58.4, 62.2) cm

21½ (23, 24½, 26, 27½, 29, 30½)" / 54.9 (58.4, 62.2, 66, 69.9, 73.7, 77.5) cm

Lace Panel Chart

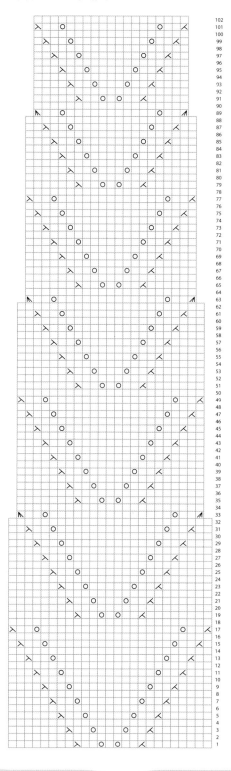

Key

☐ **Knit**
Knit on RS, Purl on WS.

⟋ **K2tog**
Knit 2 stitches together as 1 stitch
(leans right).

⟍ **SSK (modified)**
Slip 1 stitch from L to R needle knitwise.
Return stitch to L needle in its new
orientation and K2-tog through the back
loops (1 stitch decreased; leans left).

⟑ **K3tog**
Knit 3 stitches together as 1 stitch
(leans right).

◯ **Yarn over**
With yarn in front, bring yarn over top
of R needle from front to back, creating
1 new stitch.

☐ **Repeat**
Pattern repeat is indicated by red box.

Background Lace Chart
Sizes 34", 40", and 46"

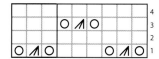

Background Lace Chart
Sizes 31", 37", 43", and 49"

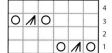

Three
SKEIN
PROJECTS

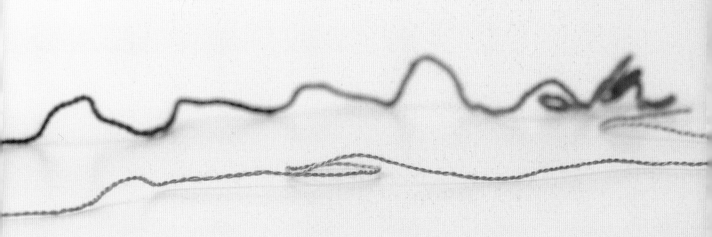

Mihika Cardigan

DESIGNER: Carol J. Sulcoski SKILL LEVEL: Intermediate

Smoky-gray lace weight yarn is knit at a relaxed gauge for this open-front cardigan, creating a fabric with suppleness and drape. Gentle pleats and bell-shaped sleeves add to the ethereal feel of this refined layering piece.

SIZES
S (M, L, 1X)

FINISHED MEASUREMENTS
Hem circumference 51½(54½, 59½, 62½)"/131 (138, 151, 159)cm

Bust circumference 37(41, 45, 49)"/94 (104, 114, 124)cm

Length from hem to shoulder 24 (24 ¼, 24 ¾, 25 ¼)"/61 (61.5, 63, 64)cm

Sleeve length to beg of cap 11 (11 ½, 12 ¼, 13)"/28 (29, 31, 33)cm

MATERIALS AND TOOLS
Ancient Arts Fibre Crafts BFL Lace (100% superwash Blue-faced Leicester wool; 3.5oz/100g = 875yd/800m): 2 (2, 2, 2) skeins, color Fog Warning—approx 1400 (1500, 1700, 1800)yd/1280 (1372, 1554, 1646)m of lace weight yarn 🧶

Knitting needles: Two 3.5mm (size 4 U.S.) 24"/60cm or 32"/80cm circular needles or size to obtain gauge

Cable needle or spare dpn

Stitch markers

Tapestry needle

GAUGE
24 sts/40 rows = 4"/10cm worked on 3.5mm (size 4 U.S.) needles in St st

Always take time to check your gauge.

PATTERN STITCHES

Double Moss Stitch (multiple of 4 sts in the round):

Rnds 1 and 2: *K2, p2, rep from * to end.

Rnds 3 and 4: *P2, k2, rep from * to end.

INSTRUCTIONS

Note: Knit the first and last st of every row to create selvedge st. Back and front pieces cast on extra stitches at bottom edge that are used to form pleats; these sts will be decreased when pleats are formed.

Back:

CO 160 (172, 184, 196) sts.

Row 1 (RS): K1, *p2, k2, rep from * to last 3 sts, p2, k1.

Row 2: K1, k the knit sts and p the purl sts to last st, k1.

Row 3: K1, *k2, p2, rep from * to last 3 sts, k3.

Row 4: Rep Row 2.

Switch to St st and work in St st, cont to k first and last st for selvedge, until back measures 8 (8 ¼, 8 ¾, 9 ¼)"/20 (21, 22, 23)cm, ending with a WS row.

Make Pleats:

K17 (22, 27, 32), slip next 8 sts onto cn and hold to front of work parallel with next 8 sts on left-hand needle; k first st from left-hand needle together with first st on cn and knit these sts together onto right-hand needle; repeat until all 8 sts from cn are used up, [k6, make another pleat holding in front] twice; k 6 (8, 10, 12); slip next 8 sts onto cnand hold in back, k the 8 sts on cn tog with next 8 sts, [k6, make another back pleat] twice, k to end—112 (124, 136, 148)sts.

Cont in St st until Back measures 14½ (14¾, 15, 15½)"/37 (37, 38, 39) cm, ending with a WS row.

Shape Armholes:

BO 6 (7, 7, 7) sts at beg of next 2 rows—100 (110, 122, 134) sts.

Dec 1 st at each end of next and every alt row a total of 5 (6, 6, 7) times.

Dec 1 st at each end of next row and every 4th row a total of 6 (6, 7, 7) times—78 (86, 96, 106) sts.

Work even until piece measures 23½ (23¾, 24¼, 24¾)"/60 (60, 62, 63)cm from beg, ending with a WS row.

Shape Shoulders:

Next 2 rows: BO 6 (6, 7, 7) sts, work to end—66 (74, 82, 92) sts.

Next row: BO 5 (6, 6, 7) sts, k to end, placing center 36 (38, 40, 44) sts on holder for back neckband.

Next row (WS): BO 5 (6, 6, 7) sts, work to end.

Work 1 row.

BO 5 (6, 6, 7) sts, work to end.

Work 1 row.

BO rem sts.

Rejoin yarn at other shoulder at neck edge, and work to match, reversing shaping.

Left Front:

Note: Stitch at right edge is always knit for selvedge st; 4 sts at left edge are kept in Double Moss Patt to form edging.

CO 75 (79, 87, 91) sts.

Row 1 (RS): K3,*p2, k2, rep from * to end.

Row 2: K the knit sts and p the purl sts to last st, k1.

Row 3: K1, p2, *k2, p2, rep from * to end.

Row 4: K the knit sts and p the purl sts to last st, k1.

Switch to St st as follows:

Row 1 (RS): K to last 4 sts, p2, k2.

Row 2: P2, k2, p to last st, k1.

Row 3: K to last 4 sts, k2, p2.

Row 4: K2, p2, p to last st, k1.

Work these 4 rows until front measures 8 (8¼, 8¾, 9¼)"/20 (21, 22, 23)cm, ending with Row 4.

Make Pleats:

Next row (RS): K29 (33, 39, 43) sts, slip next 8 sts onto cn and hold to back of work parallel with next 8 sts on left-hand needle; k first st from left-hand needle together with first st on cn and k these sts together onto right-hand needle; repeat until all 8 sts from cn are used up; k2, sl next 6 sts onto cn and make pleat in same manner; k2, slip 4 sts onto cn and make 3rd pleat in same manner; k2 (2, 4, 4), work last 4 sts in Double Moss Patt, keeping pattern as established—57 (61, 69, 73)sts.

Work in St st keeping pattern as established (i.e., knitting selvedge st on one edge and maintaining 4 edging sts in Double Moss Patt) until front measures 14½ (14¾, 15, 15½)"/37 (37, 38, 39)cm, ending with a WS row.

Shape Armhole and Neck:

Work as follows, keeping edging patt as established at all times:

Next row (RS): BO 6 (7, 7, 7) sts, work to end—51 (54, 62, 66) sts.

Work 1 row.

Dec 1 st at armhole edge of next and every other row a total of 5 (6, 6, 7) times, then dec 1 st at armhole edge of next row and every 4th row a total of 6 (6, 7, 7) times and at the same time, when armhole measures 1"/2.5cm from first set of bound-off sts, begin working neck shaping as follows:

Dec 1 st at neck edge (work dec 2 sts in from Double Moss edging) on next and every other row a total of 9 (10, 12, 13) times, then every 4th row a total of 8 (9, 8, 9) times.

When all neck and armhole edge dec are complete, 27 (27, 33, 34) sts rem.

Work even until piece measures 23½ (23¾, 24¼, 24½)"/60 (60, 62, 63)cm from beg, ending with a WS row.

Shape Shoulder:

Next row (RS): BO 6 (6, 7, 7) sts, work to end keeping patt as established—21 (21, 26, 27) sts.

Work 1 row.

Next row (RS): BO 5 (6, 6, 7) sts, work to end, keeping patt as established—16 (15, 20, 20) sts.

Work 1 row.

Next row (RS): BO 5 (6, 6, 7) sts, work to end—11 (9, 14, 13) sts.

BO rem sts.

Right Front:

Note: Stitch at left edge is always knit for selvedge st; 4 sts at right edge are kept in Double Moss Patt to form edging.

CO 75 (79, 87, 91) sts.

Row 1 (RS): *K2, p2, rep from * to last 3 sts, k3.

Row 2: K1, then k the knit sts and p the purl sts to end.

Row 3: *P2, k2, rep from * to last 3 sts, p2, k1.

Row 4: K1, then k the knit sts and p the purl sts to end.

Switch to St st as follows:

Row 1 (RS): K2, p2, k to end.

Shape Armhole and Neck:

Work as follows keeping edging patt correct at all times:

Next row (WS): BO 6 (7, 7, 7) sts, work to end—51 (54, 62, 66) sts.

Work 1 row.

Dec 1 st at armhole edge of next and every alt row a total of 5 (6, 6, 7) times, then dec 1 st at armhole edge of next row and every 4th row a total of 6 (6, 7, 7) times AND AT THE SAME TIME, when armhole measures 1"/2.5cm from first set of bound-off sts, begin working neck shaping as follows:

Dec 1 st at neck edge (work dec 2 sts in from Double Moss edging) on next and every other row a total of 5 (6, 8, 9) times, then every 4th row a total of 8 (9, 8, 9) times.

When all neck and armhole edge dec are complete, 27 (27, 33, 34) sts rem.

Work even until piece measures 23½ (23¾, 24¼, 24½)"/60 (60, 62, 63)cm from beg, ending with a RS row.

Shape Shoulder:

Next row (WS): BO 6 (6, 7, 7) sts, work to end keeping patt as established—21 (21, 26, 27) sts.

Work 1 row.

Next row (WS): BO 5 (6, 6, 7) sts, work to end, keeping pattas estab—16 (15, 20, 20) sts.

Work 1 row.

Next row (WS): BO 5 (6, 6, 7) sts, work to end—11 (9, 14, 13) sts.

BO rem sts.

Sleeves (make 2):

Flared Cuff:

CO 86 (86, 90, 90) sts.

Row 1 (RS): K1, *k2, p2, rep from * to last st, k1.

Row 2: K1, k the knit sts and p the purl sts to last st, k1.

Row 3: K1, *p2, k2, rep from * to last st, k1.

Row 4: Rep Row 2.

Row 2: K1, p to last 4 sts, k2, p2.

Row 3: P2, k2, k to end.

Row 4: K1, p to last 4 sts, p2, k2.

Work these 4 rows until front measures 8 (8¼, 8¾, 9¼)"/20 (21, 22, 23)cm, ending with Row 4.

Make Pleats:

Next row (RS): Work first 4 sts in Double Moss Patt, keeping patt as established, k2 (2, 4, 4), slip next 4 sts onto cn and hold to front of work parallel with next 4 sts on left-hand needle; k first st from left-hand needle together with first st on cn and k these sts together onto right-hand needle; repeat until all 4 sts from cn are used up; k2, sl next 6 sts onto cn and make next pleat in same manner; k2, sl next 8 sts onto cn and make last pleat in same manner; k to end—57 (61, 69, 73) sts.

Work in St st keeping patt as established (i.e., maintaining 4 edging sts in Double Moss Patt and selvedge st on side edge) until front measures 14½ (14¾, 15, 15½)"/37 (37, 38, 39)cm, ending with a RS row.

Rep last 4 rows once more.

K 1 row, then p 1 row.

Dec row (RS): K, dec 1 st at each end of sleeve—84 (84, 88, 88) sts.

Work 3 rows in St st.

Rep these 4 rows 6 more times—72 (72, 76, 76) sts.

K1 row, then p 1 row.

Main Sleeve Section:

Next row (RS): K, inc 1 st at each end of row—74 (74, 78, 78) sts.

Work 5 rows in St st.

Rep these 6 rows 4 (4, 5, 5) more times—82 (82, 88, 88) sts.

Next row (RS): K, inc 1 st at each end of row—84 (84, 90, 90) sts.

Work 3 rows in St st.

Rep these 4 rows 3 (4, 4, 6) more times—90 (92, 98, 102) sts.

Work even in St st until sleeve measures 11 (11½, 12¼, 13)"/28 (29, 31, 33)cm, ending with a WS row.

Shape Cap:

BO 6 (7, 7, 7) sts at beg of next 2 rows—78 (78, 84, 88) sts.

BO 2 sts at beg of next 4 rows—70 (70, 76, 80) sts.

Next row (RS): Dec 1 st at each end of row—68 (68, 74, 78) sts.

Next row: Purl.

Rep these 2 rows 4 (4, 5, 5) more times—60 (60, 64, 68) sts.

*BO 2 sts at beg of next 2 rows, then work 0 (2, 2, 2) rows even.

Dec 1 st at each end of next row.

Work 1 row even.**

Rep from * to ** 1 more time—48 (48, 52, 56) sts.

Dec 1 st at each end of next row—46 (46, 50, 54) sts.

Work 1 row.

Rep these 2 rows 2 (2, 3, 4) more times—42 (42, 44, 46) sts.

BO 2 sts at beg of next 6 rows—30 (30, 32, 34) sts.

BO 3 sts at beg of next 4 rows—18 (18, 20, 22) sts.

BO rem 18 (18, 20, 22) sts.

FINISHING

Sew shoulders together, beginning after Double Moss edging on each front piece, easing to fit if necessary. Set in sleeves and sew sleeve and side seams.

Neckband:

Beg at right front, with RS of cardigan facing knitter, pick up 5 sts across top of Double Moss edging, pick up 11 (12, 15, 17) sts across right back neck edge, knit across center 36 (38, 40, 44) from holder, pick up 11 (13, 15, 17) sts across leftback neck edge, pick up 5 sts across top of Double Moss edging—68 (72, 80, 88) sts.

Row 1 (WS): *K2, p2, rep from * to end.

Row 2: K the knit sts and p the purl sts.

Row 3: *P2, k2, rep from * to end.

Row 4: K the knit sts and p the purl sts..

BO all sts knitwise.

Schematics

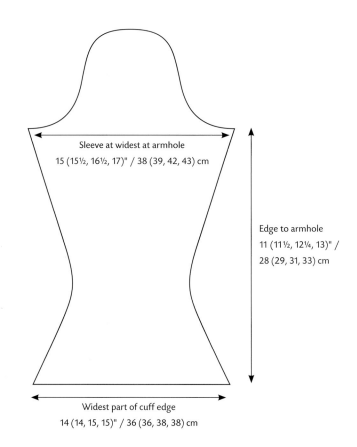

Sleeve at widest at armhole
15 (15½, 16½, 17)" / 38 (39, 42, 43) cm

Edge to armhole
11 (11½, 12¼, 13)" / 28 (29, 31, 33) cm

Widest part of cuff edge
14 (14, 15, 15)" / 36 (36, 38, 38) cm

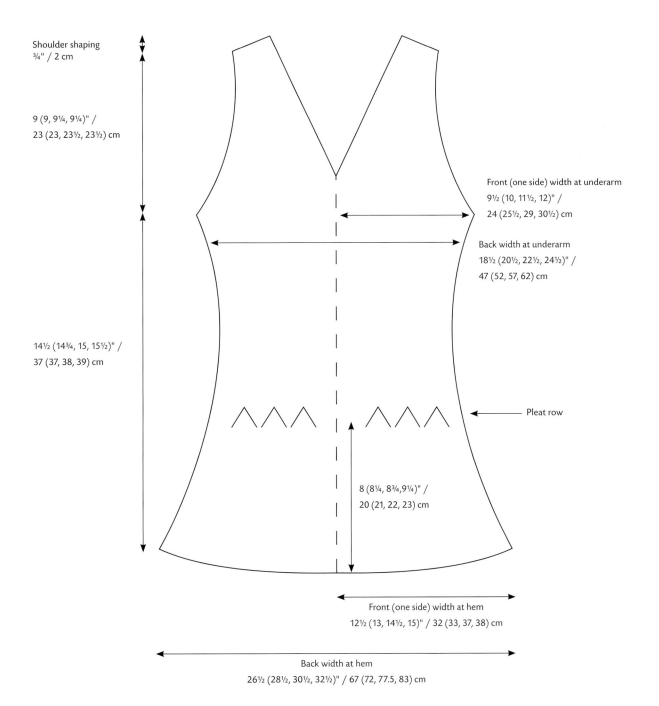

Shoulder shaping
¾" / 2 cm

9 (9, 9¼, 9¼)" /
23 (23, 23½, 23½) cm

Front (one side) width at underarm
9½ (10, 11½, 12)" /
24 (25½, 29, 30½) cm

Back width at underarm
18½ (20½, 22½, 24½)" /
47 (52, 57, 62) cm

14½ (14¾, 15, 15½)" /
37 (37, 38, 39) cm

Pleat row

8 (8¼, 8¾, 9¼)" /
20 (21, 22, 23) cm

Front (one side) width at hem
12½ (13, 14½, 15)" / 32 (33, 37, 38) cm

Back width at hem
26½ (28½, 30½, 32½)" / 67 (72, 77.5, 83) cm

Audrey Beaded Skirt

DESIGNER: Barbara J. Brown SKILL LEVEL: Easy

This gored skirt has a little bit of flash and a lot of class. You'll love the way it swings and flows as you walk or stroll, dressed up for the town, or dressed down for a walk in the park, adding a touch of elegance to your everyday life.

SIZES
S (M, L, 1X, 2X, 3X)

FINISHED MEASUREMENTS
Waist 29¾ (33½, 37, 40¼, 45¾, 48¼)"/76 (85, 94, 102, 116, 123)cm

To fit waist 26¾ (30, 33, 36¼, 41, 43¼)"/68 (76, 84, 92, 104, 110)cm

---

MATERIALS AND TOOLS
Valley Yarns Colrain Lace (50% merino/50% Tencel; 8.8oz/250g = 1540yd/1408m): 1 (2, 2, 2, 2, 2) cones, color Coffee—approx 1650 (1850, 2050, 2250, 2550, 2700)yd/1509 (1692, 1875, 2057, 2332, 2469)m of laceweight yarn

Knitting needles: 3.75mm (size 5 U.S.) 24"/60cm or 32"/80cm (depending on skirt size) circular needle or size to obtain gauge

Approx 400 size 6/0 (3mm) seed beads

8 stitch markers

0.75mm (size 14 U.S.) steel crochet hook (for attaching beads)

Tapestry needle

Length of ¾"/19mm waistband elastic approx 2"/5cm smaller than actual waist size

GAUGE
26 sts/36 rows = 4"/10cm in St st using single strand

Always take time to check your gauge.

SPECIAL ABBREVIATIONS
M1L (Make One Left) – With left needle tip, lift strand between needles from front to back. K the lifted strand through the back.

M1R (Make One Right) – With left needle tip, lift strand between needles from back to front. K the lifted strand through the front.

PB (Place Bead) – Place a bead on crochet hook. Slip next st from left-hand needle onto crochet hook; pull st through bead and place st on right-hand needle. On next rnd, work beaded st as usual.

INSTRUCTIONS

Note: Skirt is knit from the top down circularly. Waistband is knit with yarn held double; remainder of skirt is knit with single strand of yarn.

Knit 1 rnd, inc 6 (6, 8, 2, 6, 6) sts evenly around—200 (224, 248, 264, 304, 320) sts.

Place markers to show gores:

Next rnd: *K25 (28, 31, 33, 38, 40), pm; rep from * to last 25 (28, 31, 33, 38, 40) sts, k to end.

Knit 5 rnds.

Incrnd: *K1, M1L, k to marker, M1R, sl marker; rep from * to end—216 (240, 264, 280, 320, 336) sts.

Knit 16 rnds.

Work Inc Rnd.

Rep portion between brackets until there are 43 (46, 49, 51, 56, 58) sts between markers, or skirt is 13"/33cm less than desired finished length.

Add Beads:

Knit 16 rnds, PB on first st after each marker on Rnds 2, 6, 10, and 14 (or use Chart A for bead placement).

Work Inc Rnd—360 (384, 408, 424, 464, 480) sts.

Rep these 17 rnds 3 more times.

Knit 16 rnds, PB on 2nd st before marker, first st after marker and 3rd st after marker on Rnds 2, 6, 10, and 14 (or use Chart B for bead placement).

Work Inc Rnd—376 (400, 424, 440, 480, 496) sts.

Knit 16 rnds, PB on 4th st before marker, 2nd st before marker, first st after marker, 3rd st after marker, and 5th st after marker, on Rnds 2, 6, 10, and 14 (or use Chart C for bead placement).

Work Inc Rnd—392 (416, 440, 456, 496, 512) sts.

Purl 1 rnd (to create turning ridge for hem).

Knit 8 rnds.

BO all sts. (Note: If desired, bottom of hem can be joined to 8th rnd from end by using 3-needle bind-off, but if hem comes undone, skirt may ravel.)

FINISHING

Weave in all ends and block as desired. If necessary, sew waistband casing to inside of skirt, leaving opening of approx 3"/8cm to insert elastic. Insert waistband elastic in desired length and sew carefully to inside casing. Turn hem and sew to inside of skirt.

Waistband:

With 2 strands of yarn held tog, CO 194 (218, 240, 262, 298, 314) sts. Join for knitting in the rnd, being careful not to twist, and place st marker to show beg of rnd.

Knit 6 rnds.

Purl 1 rnd (to create turning ridge).

Knit 6 rnds.

Optional rnd: *K next st and pass working yarn through loop of corresponding st of cast-on edge; rep from * to last 15 sts, k15. (If desired, omit this round and sew waistband casing when skirt is complete.)

Skirt:

Break off one strand of yarn and continue using single strand.

Chart A

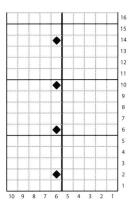

Key

| ◆ | place bead |
| marker position |

Chart B

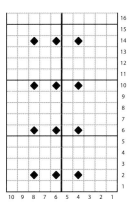

Chart C

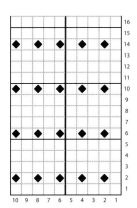

Cobalt Nights Sleeveless Jacket

DESIGNER: Brooke Nico   SKILL LEVEL: Easy

Lace weight yarns can be ethereal and delicate—but they can also be bold and metallic, like this glittery rayon blend in a deep shade of blue. Drape, swing, shine, this sleeveless garment's got it all

SIZES
S (M, L/1X)

FINISHED MEASUREMENTS
Bust 36 (40, 46)"/91 (102, 117)cm

Length 30"/76cm

MATERIALS AND TOOLS
S. Charles Collezione Celine (60% rayon/40% metallic; 0.71oz/20g = 163yd/149m): 6 (6, 7) balls, color #10—approx 978 (978, 1141)yd/894 (894, 1043)m of lace weight yarn

Knitting needles: 4.5mm (size 7 U.S.) or size to obtain gauge

Coiless safety pins

Yarn needle

GAUGE
20 sts/38 rows = 4"/10cm over Star Stitch patterns, washed and blocked

Always take time to check your gauge.

SPECIAL ABBREVIATIONS
2/2R – K2tog but do not drop sts off left needle, knit the same 2 sts together through the back loops, drop sts off left needle.

2/2L – K2tog-tbl but do not drop sts off left needle, k the same 2 sts together through the front loops, drop sts off left needle.

PATTERN STITCHES

Star Stitch Left (multiple of 2 sts):

Row 1 (RS): K1, *2/2L; rep from * to last st, k1.

Row 2: Purl.

Row 3: K2, *2/2L; rep from * to last 2 sts, k2.

Row 4: Purl.

Rep Rows 1–4 for Star Stitch Left patt.

Star Stitch Right (multiple of 2 sts):

Row 1 (RS): K1, *2/2R; rep from * to last st, k1.

Row 2: Purl.

Row 3: K2, *2/2R; rep from * to last 2 sts, k2.

Row 4: Purl.

Rep Rows 1–4 for Star Stitch Right patt.

INSTRUCTIONS

Notes: The 2/2 cross-stitch is a stitch found often in Estonian lace motifs. In this vest, we're using it as an all-over pattern, which resembles twinkling stars. As an all-over motif, however, this stitch will create a slow bias. Switching the order of the cross-stitches at the center back takes advantage of this bias to create a smooth-fitting neckline. This is a very elastic stitch pattern. When measuring length within the pattern, always measure with the fabric slightly stretched.

Beg at right front edge, CO 150 sts.

Work in Star Stitch Left patt until piece measures about 11 (12, 14)"/28 (30, 36) cm from cast-on edge, end with a Row 4 of patt.

Right Armhole:

Next row: K1, [2/2L] 15 times, BO next 41 sts, *2/2L; rep from * to last st, k1.

Next row: P78, CO 41 sts, p to end of row.

Right Back:

Work Star Stitch Left patt Rows 3 and 4 once, then rep rows 1–4 of patt until piece measures 7 (8, 9)"/18 (20, 23) cm from armhole, end with a Row 4 of patt. Place coiless safety pin at the beg of next row for center back.

Left Back:

Work in Star Stitch Right patt until piece measures 7 (8, 9)"/18 (20, 23)cm from center back, end with a Row 4 of patt.

Left Armhole:

Next row: K1, [2/2R] 15 times, BO next 41 sts, *2/2R; rep from * to last st, k1.

Next row: P78, CO 41 sts, p to end of row.

Left Front:

Work Star Stitch Right patt Rows 3 and 4 once, then rep Rows 1–4 until piece measures 11 (12, 14)"/28 (30, 36) cm from armhole, end with a Row 4 of patt.

BO loosely knitwise.

FINISHING

Weave in all ends.

Block piece to measurements.

Schematic

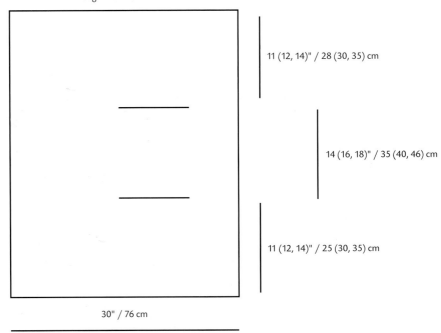

Right front–bind off

11 (12, 14)" / 28 (30, 35) cm

14 (16, 18)" / 35 (40, 46) cm

11 (12, 14)" / 25 (30, 35) cm

30" / 76 cm

Left front–cast on

Multiply Baby Blanket

DESIGNER: Carol J. Sulcoski SKILL LEVEL: Easy

For a long time, I've been fascinated by playing with plies—stranding two or more yarns together to create interesting color or textural effects. Lace weight yarn is fine enough that I chose to knit three strands together, changing colors one strand at a time, for softly-shaded color changes. This blanket is knit in the round, from the center out, and I opted for some nontraditional colors for baby using a butter-soft alpaca/merino blend.

FINISHED MEASUREMENTS
Diameter 34"/86cm diameter, after blocking

MATERIALS AND TOOLS
Rowan Fine Lace (80% baby suri alpaca/20% fine merino; 1.75oz/50g = 437yd/400m): (A), 3 skeins, color Cameo (beige) #920; (B), 1 skein, color Renaissance (warm red) #937; (C), 1 skein, color Leaf (green) #931; (D), 1 skein, color Aged (teal) #933; (E), 1 skein, color Festival (orange) #939; (F) 1 skein, color Sonata (dark purple) #940—approx 750 yd/686m of lace weight yarn in color (A) and 250yd/229m of lace weight yarn in each of 5 contrast colors

Knitting needles: Two 3.5mm (size 4 U.S.) 32"/80cm circular needles or size to obtain gauge

Waste yarn (for provisional cast-on)

8 stitch markers

Tapestry needle

GAUGE
20sts/24 rows = 4"/10cm in St st using 3 strands of yarn held together

Always take time to check your gauge.

SPECIAL ABBREVIATIONS
Kfb (knit into front and back) – Knit into the front and back of the next stitch—inc 1 st.

M1L (Make One Left) – With left needle tip, lift strand between needles from front to back. K the lifted strand through the back.

M1R (Make One Right) – With left needle tip, lift strand between needles from back to front. K the lifted strand through the front.

INSTRUCTIONS

Notes:

1. Blanket begins by using a provisional cast-on with waste yarn. When blanket is finished, provisional cast-on is removed and yarn is fastened off.

2. Blanket is knit in the rnd, from the center out. Because circumference is small at beg of patt, use your preferred method of knitting smaller circumferences in the rnd (2 circulars, dpns, or magic loop method; instructions are written for 2-circular method). As blanket gets larger, transfer to a single circular needle with sufficiently long cable to hold sts.

Using waste yarn, CO 8 sts.

Work in I-cord for approx 1½"/4cm, then break off waste yarn.

Using 3 strands of A held together, knit 1 rnd.

Now join for knitting in the rnd, being careful not to twist.

Rnd 1: *Kfb; rep from * to end—16 sts.

Rnd 2: Knit.

Rnd 3: *K1, kfb; rep from * to end—24 sts.

Rnd 4: K1, pm, *k3, pm; rep from * to last 2 sts, k2.

Inc Rnd: *K to marker, M1L, sl marker, k1, M1R, k2; rep from * to last 2 sts, k2—40 sts.

Rnds 2–4: Knit.

Rep these 4 rnds until blanket measures 2"/5cm from center, ending with a Rnd 2.

Break off 1 strand of A and replace with 1 strand of B. Cont working, keeping patt correct, until this section measures 1¼"/3cm.

Break off 1 strand of A and replace with another strand of B. Cont until this section measures 1"/2.5cm.

Cont in this manner, always working increases on every 4th rnd, and changing color as in the following chart (always change colors on a Rnd 3):

Colors:	Length of section:
3 strands B	1¼"/3cm
1 strand C/2 strands B	½"/1cm
2 strands C/1 strand B	1¼"/3cm
3 strands C	½"/1cm
1 strand D/2 strands C	1¼"/3cm
2 strands D/1 strand C	½"/1cm
3 strands D	1"/2.5cm
1 strand E/2 strands D	½"/1cm
2 strands E/1 strand D	1"/2.5cm
3 strands E	½"/1cm
1 strand F/2 strands E	½"/1cm
2 strands F/1 strand E	½"/1cm
3 strands F	1¼"/3cm
3 strands A	1¼"/3cm

Edging:

When you have finished working 1¼"/3cm of last section (in 3 strands of A), work edging of blanket with 3 strands of A held together, as follows: Knit 1 rnd, rep Inc Rnd. Now work ¾"/2cm in Garter st (knit 1 rnd, purl 1 rnd), and BO all sts loosely.

FINISHING

Carefully remove waste yarn from provisional cast-on, placing 8 live sts on spare needle; thread tail of yarn through tapestry needle and fasten off sts. Weave in ends and block.

Coaxial Baby Cap

DESIGNER: Carol J. Sulcoski SKILL LEVEL: Easy

Lace weight yarns are perfect for gathering, ruffling, and tucking—and ruching is an easy way to get this delightful effect with a minimum of fuss. This baby cap uses small amounts of lace weight yarn in a variety of colors (left over from the Multiply Baby Blanket) to create ruched stripes on a background of soft fingering weight yarn.

SIZES
For sizes 12 mo. (2-4T, 6 yrs)

FINISHED MEASUREMENTS
Circumference 15¼ (16½, 17¾)"/39 (42, 45)cm

MATERIALS AND TOOLS
Schachenmayr Regia Silk (55% merino/25% nylon/20% silk; 1.76oz/50g = 219yd/200m): 1 skein, color Linen Marl #00005—approx 150–200yd/137–183m of fingering weight yarn (1)

Rowan Fine Lace (80% baby suri alpaca/20% merino; 1.75oz/50g = 437yd/400m): small amount each of #00927 (A), #00939 (B), and #00933 (C)—approx 30–50yd/27–46m each of three lace weight yarns (0)

Knitting needles: 3.25mm (size 3 U.S.) 16"/40cm circular needle or size to obtain gauge

3.25mm (size 3 U.S.) dpns or second circular needle

2.75mm (size 2 U.S.) 16"/40cm circular needle or one size smaller than above

Stitch marker

Tapestry needle

GAUGE

26 sts/32 rnds = 4"/10cm using (MC) on 3mm (size 3 U.S.) in St st

Always take time to check your gauge.

SPECIAL ABBREVIATION

Kfb (knit into front and back) – Knit into the front and back of the next stitch–inc 1 st.

PATTERN STITCH

Double Seed Stitch (multiple of 4 sts; in the rnd):

Rnds 1 and 2: *K2, p2, rep from * to end.

Rnds 3 and 4: *P2, k2, rep from * to end.

INSTRUCTIONS

Using MC and 2.75mm (size 2 U.S.) needle, CO 100 (108, 116) sts. PM and join for knitting in the rnd, being careful not to twist.

Work in Double Seed Stitch until cap measures 1"/2.5cm from beg, ending with a Rnd 2 or 4.

Switch to larger needle and with MC knit for an additional ¾ (¾, 1)"/2 (2, 3)cm.

Switch to A and smaller needle and knit 1 rnd.

Next rnd: *Kfb, rep to end–200 (216, 232) sts.

K 6 rnds.

Next rnd: *K2tog, rep to end–100 (108, 116) sts.

Rep section between brackets once using B then once using C.

Switch to MC and larger needle and knit for an additional ¾ (1, 1)"/2 (3, 3) cm.

Shape Crown:

Rnd 1: *K4, k2tog, rep from * to last 4 (0, 2)sts, k4 (0, 2)–84 (90, 97) sts.

Rnd 2: Knit.

Rnd 3: *K3, k2tog, rep from * to last 2 sts, k4 (0, 2)–68 (72, 78) sts.

Rnd 4: Knit.

Rnd 5: *K2, k2tog, rep from * to last 0 (0, 2) sts, k0 (0, 2)–51 (54, 59) sts.

Rnd 6: Knit.

Rnd 7: *K1, k2tog, rep from * to last 0 (0, 2) sts, k0 (0, 2)–34 (36, 38) sts.

Rnd 8: Knit.

Rnd 9: *K2tog, rep from * to end–17 (18, 19) sts.

Rnd 10: *K2tog, rep from * to last 1 (0, 1) st, k 1 (0, 1)–9 (9, 10) sts.

Break yarn and pull through rem sts.

FINISHING

Weave in all ends and gently steam block.

Metallique Necklace

DESIGNER: Carol J. Sulcoski SKILL LEVEL: Easy

Leftover balls of yarn are too good to waste: use them to create quick and easy I-cords that combine into necklaces. Just twist or braid and you're good to go.

FINISHED MEASUREMENTS
Length 24"/61cm

MATERIALS AND TOOLS
Habu Textiles Cotton Nerimaki Slub (100% cotton; 0.85oz/24g = 158yd/97m): (A), 1 skein, color khaki #6; (B), 1 skein, color gray #8; (C), 1 skein, color orange #1—approx 40yd/36m of each of 3 colors of lace weight yarn 🔵

Knitting needles: 3.25mm (size 3 U.S.) dpns or circular needle

Waste yarn (for provisional cast-on)

Tapestry needle

GAUGE
32 sts/36 rows = 4"/10cm in St st

Always take time to check your gauge.

INSTRUCTIONS

*Using waste yarn and provisional cast-on, CO 5 sts.

Switch to A and work in I-cord for 24"/61cm or desired length.

Cut yarn, leaving about 18"/46cm tail.**

Graft live sts from provisional cast-on to sts on needle.

Rep from * to ** using B.

Twist second I-cord around first, then graft live sts from provisional cast-on to sts on needle.

Rep from * to ** again using C. Hold first two I-cords together, as if a single strand, and twist third I-cord around them, then graft live sts from provisional cast-on to sts on needle.

FINISHING

Weave in all ends.

Graciela Pullover

DESIGNER: Carol J. Sulcoski   SKILL LEVEL: Easy

Nothing beats superfine yarn for creating sheer, lightweight layering pieces. This knit-in-the-round pullover is designed for a body-hugging fit. It features three shades of a gorgeous handpainted yarn and an easy-to-work drop stitch—the results are drop-dead gorgeous!

SIZES
S (M, L, 1X, 2X, 3X)

FINISHED MEASUREMENTS
Bust circumference 34¼ (37¾, 41¼, 44½, 48, 51½)"/87 (96, 105, 113, 122, 131)cm

Length (shoulder to hem) 21½ (22¼, 23¼, 23¾, 24¾, 26)"/55 (56.5, 59, 60.5, 63, 66)cm, including neckband

Note: Sweater is designed to be worn with a minimal amount of ease.

MATERIALS AND TOOLS
Fiesta Yarns Gracie's Lace (70% extrafine merino/15% cashmere/15% silk; 3.5oz/100g = 960yd/878m): (A), 1 skein, color Moulin Rouge (semisolid red); (B), 1 skein, color Rhubarb (multicolor); (C), 1 skein, color Cajeta (semisolid gold)—approx 300 (340, 380, 430, 480, 530)yd/274 (311, 347, 393, 439, 485)m each of 3 colors of lace weight yarn (900[1020, 1140, 1290, 1440, 1590]yd/823 [933, 1042, 1180, 1317, 1454]m total) (0)

Knitting needles: 5.5mm (size 9 U.S.) 32"/80cm circular needle or size to obtain gauge

16"/40 cm circular needle in same size

Stitch markers

Spare needle or stitch holder

Tapestry needle

GAUGE
14 sts/27 rnds = 4"/10cm worked on 5.5mm (size 9 U.S.) needles in Dropped Stitch Stripe Patt, after blocking

Always take time to check your gauge.

SPECIAL ABBREVIATION
Kfb–Knit in the front and back of st—1 st inc'd.

PATTERN STITCHES

Dropped Stitch Stripe Patt (in the round):

Rnds 1 and 3: With A, knit.

Rnds 2 and 4: With A, purl.

Rnd 5: With B, knit, wrapping yarn twice around needle for each st.

Rnd 6: With B, purl, dropping extra loops.

Rnd 7: With B, knit.

Rnd 8: With B, purl.

Rnd 9: With C, knit.

Rnd 10: with C, purl.

Rnd 11: With C, knit, wrapping yarn twice around needle for each st.

Rnd 12: With C, purl, dropping extra loops.

Dropped Stitch Stripe Patt (back-and-forth):

Rows 1–4: With A, knit.

Row 5: With B, knit, wrapping yarn twice around needle for each st.

Row 6: With B, knit, dropping extra loops.

Rows 7 and 8: With B, knit.

Rows 9 and 10: With C, knit.

Row 11: With C, knit, wrapping yarn twice around needle for each st.

Row 12: With C, knit, dropping extra loops.

INSTRUCTIONS

Note: Sweater is knit in the round from the bottom up beg with body; sleeves are knit separately and then joined to body for raglan shaping.

Body:

With A, CO 120 (132, 144, 156, 168, 180) sts using knit cast-on. Join for working in the round, being careful not to twist; place marker to show beg of rnd.

Rnd 1: Knit.

Rnd 2: Purl.

Rnd 3: Knit.

Rnd 4: Purl.

Begin Dropped Stitch Stripe Patt and work until body measures 14 (14¼, 14½, 15, 16, 17)"/36 (36, 38, 38, 41, 43)cm from beg, ending with a Rnd 2 and ending last rnd without working last 3 (3, 3, 4, 4, 4) sts of rnd. BO last 3 (3, 3, 4, 4, 4) sts of this rnd.

Next rnd: BO 3 (3, 3, 4, 4, 4) sts, work until there are 54 (60, 66, 70, 76, 82) sts on right-hand needle, BO 6 (6, 6, 8, 8, 8) sts, work to end. Set work aside.

Sleeves:

With A, CO 28 (28, 30, 32, 32, 34) sts using knit cast-on or other elastic cast-on. Join for working in the round, being careful not to twist, place marker to show beg of rnd.

Rnd 1: Knit.

Rnd 2: Purl.

Rnd 3: Knit.

Rnd 4: Purl.

Work Rnds 1–6 of Dropped Stitch Stripe Patt.

Beg with Rnd 7 of stitch pattern, inc at beg and end of this and every 6th rnd a total of 8 (7, 8, 8, 8, 9) times, then every 4th rnd a total of 0 (2, 3, 3, 4, 3) times—44 (46, 52, 54, 56, 58) sts.

Cont without further shaping until sleeve measures approx 12½ (13¼, 14¼, 15¼, 16¾, 18)"/32 (34, 36, 39, 43, 46)cm or desired length to armhole, ending with a Rnd 2 and ending last rnd without working last 3 (3, 3, 4, 4, 4) sts of rnd. BO last 3 (3, 3, 4, 4, 4) sts of this rnd.

Next rnd: BO 3 (3, 3, 4, 4, 4) sts and work to end—38 (40, 46, 46, 48, 50) sts. Place live sts on spare needle or stitch holder and set aside.

Make second sleeve to match.

Join Body and Sleeves:

Keeping pattern as established (you will be starting on a Rnd 4), work across 38 (40, 46, 46, 48, 50) sts of one sleeve, pm, work across 54 (60, 66, 70, 76, 82) front sts, pm, work across 38 (40, 46, 46, 48, 50) sts of second sleeve, pm, work across 54 (60, 66, 70, 76, 82) back sts, place different colored marker to show beg of rnd—184 (200, 224, 232, 248, 264) sts.

Raglan dec rnd: Work next rnd of pattern, dec 1 st before and after each marker (8 sts dec over entire rnd).

Work next rnd of patt.

Rep these 2 rnds 16 (17, 18, 18, 19, 20) more times and AT THE SAME TIME, when sweater measures 5½ (5¾, 6, 6, 6, 6 ¼)"/14 (15, 15, 15, 15, 16)cm from where sleeves are joined, begin working neck as follows (Note: For best results, BO center neck sts on a Rnd 1, 3, 7, or 9 of patt):

BO center 10 (12, 12, 14, 14, 16) sts of front for neck, work to end of rnd.

Note: Rnd now begins at neck edge.

Now working back and forth, switching to back-and-forth version of Dropped Stitch Stripe Patt, and continuing to work rem raglan dec, BO 2 sts at each neck edge on next 2 (2, 3, 3, 3, 3) RS rows, then dec 1 st at each neck edge on following1 (2, 3, 3, 3,3) RS rows—28 (32, 42, 48, 56, 62) sts rem.

Neckband:

With A, knit across 28 (32, 42, 48, 56, 62) live sts on needle, then pick up and knit 22 (32, 42, 48, 56, 62)sts across BO neck sts.

Join for working in the rnd and place marker to show beg of rnd.

P 1 rnd.

K 1 rnd, then p 1 rnd; rep these 2 rnds once more.

BO all sts using elastic bind-off such as sewn bind-off.

FINISHING

Weave in ends; carefully sew opening under each armhole. Block gently as desired.

Schematic

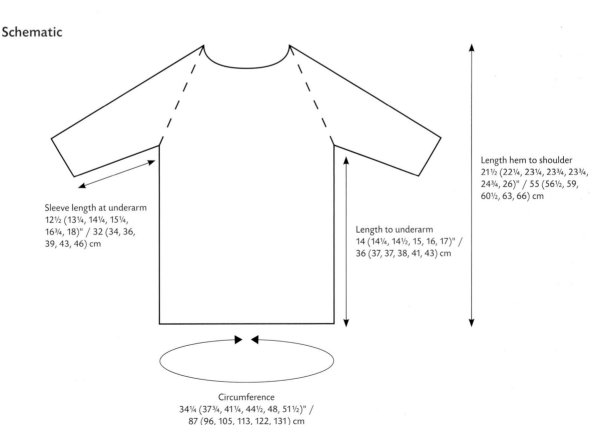

Sleeve length at underarm
12½ (13¼, 14¼, 15¼, 16¾, 18)" / 32 (34, 36, 39, 43, 46) cm

Length to underarm
14 (14¼, 14½, 15, 16, 17)" / 36 (37, 37, 38, 41, 43) cm

Length hem to shoulder
21½ (22¼, 23¼, 23¾, 23¾, 24¾, 26)" / 55 (56½, 59, 60½, 63, 66) cm

Circumference
34¼ (37¾, 41¼, 44½, 48, 51½)" / 87 (96, 105, 113, 122, 131) cm

Aileana Vest

DESIGN BY Fiona Ellis SKILL LEVEL: Intermediate

Cables and eyelets embellish this elegant vest, perfect for layering and wearing all year-round.
A chiffon ribbon is a delightful touch, although you can use knitted I-cord if you prefer.

SIZES
XS (S, M, L, 1X, 2X)

FINISHED MEASUREMENTS
Bust 32½ (35½, 38½, 42½, 45½, 48½)"/83 (90, 98, 108, 116, 123)cm

Length 22 (22½, 23, 24, 25, 26)"/56 (57, 58, 61, 64, 66)cm

MATERIALS AND TOOLS
Black Bunny Fibers Heavenly Lace (70% baby alpaca/20% silk/10% cashmere; 3.5oz/100g = 1300yd/1189m): 1 (2, 2, 2, 2, 2) skeins, color Dead Presidents—approx 1250 (1400, 1550, 1800, 2000, 2200)yd/1143 (1280, 1417, 1646, 1829, 2012)m of lace weight yarn 🧶

Knitting needles: 3.5mm (size 4 U.S.) 32"/80cm circular needle or size to obtain gauge

3.5mm (size 4 U.S.) dpns (optional; if working I-cord ties)

Cable needle

Stitch holders

3yd/2.75m of 1"/25mm-wide ribbon; sample used ombré chiffon ribbon (optional; if desired, ribbon can be replaced by I-cord ties)

Size 3.25mm (size D/3 U.S.) crochet hook for securing back neck

GAUGE
32sts/36 rows = 4"/10cm in St st

Lace Eyelet Panel = 5½"/13cm wide

Notes:
BO all sts loosely as follows:

K2, *slip these sts back onto left-hand needle and k2tog, k1, rep from * to end.

SPECIAL ABBREVIATIONS
C4B – Slip next 2 sts onto cn and hold at back, k2 from left needle, k 2 sts from cn.

Cdd (Centered double decrease) – Slip 2 sts as if to k2tog, k1, psso.

PATTERN STITCHES

Honeybee Pattern (panel of 12 sts):

Row 1 (RS): K4, k2tog, yo, ssk, k4.

Row 2: P3, p2tog-tbl, drop yo from previous row from the needle, (yo) twice, p2tog, p3.

Row 3: K2, k2tog, drop double yo from previous row from the needle, (yo) 3 times, ssk, k2.

Row 4: P1, p2tog-tbl, drop triple yo from previous row from the needle, (yo) 4 times, p2tog, p1.

Row 5: K2tog, drop the yo's from previous row from the needle, cast on 4 sts to right needle, take tip of right needle, working from front to back, down under the 4 strands made by the yo's on previous rows and draw up loop as if to k, yo, k1 again under yo strands, cast on 4 sts to right needle, ssk.

Row 6: P5, p2tog-tbl, p6.

Rep Rows 1–6 for Honeybee Patt.

Lace Eyelet Pattern (panel of 36 sts):

Row 1: K5, (k2tog, yo, k4) 4 times, k2tog, yo, k5.

Row 2 and all WS rows: Purl all sts.

Row 3: K10, k2tog, yo, k1, yo, ssk, k7, k2tog, yo, k1, yo, ssk, k9.

Row 5: K11, yo, cdd, yo, k9, yo, cdd, yo, k10.

Row 7: Rep Row 5.

Row 9: Rep Row 1.

Row 11: K4, (k2tog, yo, k1, yo, ssk, k7) twice, k2tog, yo, k1, yo, ssk, k3.

Row 13: K5, (yo, cdd, yo, k9) twice, yo, cdd, yo, k4.

Row 15: Rep Row 13.

Row 16: Rep Row 2.

Rep Rows 1–16 for Lace Eyelet Patt.

Cable Pattern (multiple of 6 sts + 2):

Row 1(RS): P2, *k4, p2; rep from * to end.

Row 2: *K2, p4; rep from * to last 2 sts, k2.

Row 3: P2, *C4B, p2; rep from * to end.

Row 4: Rep Row 2.

Rows 5 and 6: Rep Rows 1 and 2.

Rep rows 1–6 for Cable Patt.

Seed Stitch (even number of stitches):

Row 1: (K1, p1) to end.

Row 2: (P1, k1) to end.

Rep Rows 1 and 2 for Seed st.

I-cord (optional):

Using a pair of double pointed needles (dpns), cast on 4 sts and knit them. *Do not turn the needle. Simply slide the sts to the opposite end of needle, pull the yarn across the back of the sts and knit them once more*. Repeat from * to * until desired length.

INSTRUCTIONS

Note: Vest is knit flat throughout; circular needles are used to hold large number of stitches.

Using circular needle, CO 260 (284, 308, 340, 364, 388) sts.

Working flat throughout, work 3 rows in Seed st.

Set-up row (WS): P0 (0, 0, 4, 4, 4), *(k2, p4) 3 (4, 5, 6, 7, 8) times, k2, (p12, k2, p4, k2) 3 times, p12, (k2, p4) 3 (4, 5, 6, 7, 8) times, k2 **, p36, rep from * to **, p0 (0, 0, 4, 4) times.

Establish Patterns:

Row 1 (RS): K0 (0, 0, 4, 4, 4), following Row 1 for all patts; work Cable Patt over next 20 (26, 32, 38, 44, 50) sts, (work Honeybee Patt over next 12 sts, work Cable Patt over foll 8 sts) 3 times, work Honeybee Patt over next 12 sts, work Cable Patt over next 20 (26, 32, 38, 44, 50) sts, work 3 reps of Honeybee Pattover next 36 sts, work Cable Patt over next 20 (26, 32, 38, 44, 50) sts, (work Honeybee Patt over next 12 sts, work Cable Patt over foll 8 sts) 3 times, work Honeybee Patt, work Cable Patt over next 20 (26, 32, 38, 44, 50) sts, k0 (0, 0, 4, 4, 4).

Row 2 (WS): P0 (0, 0, 4, 4, 4), following Row 2 for all patts; work Cable Patt over next 20 (26, 32, 38, 44, 50) sts, (work Honeybee Patt over next 12 sts, work Cable Patt over foll 8 sts) 3 times, work Honeybee Patt over next 12 sts, work Cable Patt over next 20 (26, 32, 38, 44, 50) sts, work 3 reps of Honeybee Patt over next 36 sts, work Cable Patt over next 20 (26, 32, 38, 44, 50) sts, (work Honeybee Patt over next 12 sts, work Cable Patt over foll 8 sts) 3 times, work Honeybee Patt, work Cable Patt over next 20 (26, 32, 38, 44, 50) sts, p0 (0, 0, 4, 4, 4).

Cont working patts in sequence, until 3 reps of Honeybee Patt (a total of 18 pattern rows) have been completed.

Cont, working Cable Patt as established and work the following Lace Eyelet Patt in place of all Honeybee Patts.

Row 1 (RS): K5, k2tog, yo, k5.

Row 2 and all WS rows: Purl all sts.

Row 3: K4, k2tog, yo, k1, yo, ssk, k3.

Row 5: K5, yo, cdd, yo, k4.

Row 7: Rep Row 5.

Row 8: Rep Row 2.

Next row (RS): K0 (0, 0, 4, 4, 4), following Row 1 for all patts; work Cable Patt over next 20 (26, 32, 38, 44, 50) sts, (k5, k2tog, yo, k5, work Cable Patt over foll 8 sts) 3 times, work k5, k2tog, yo, k5, work Cable Patt over next 20 (26, 32, 38, 44, 50) sts, work Row 1 Lace Eyelet Patt over next 36 sts, work Cable Patt over next 20 (26, 32, 38, 44, 50) sts, (k5, k2tog, yo, k5, work Cable Patt over foll 8 sts) 3 times, k5, k2tog, yo, k5, work Cable Patt over next 20 (26, 32, 38, 44, 50) sts, k0 (0, 0, 4, 4, 4).

Next row (WS): P0 (0, 0, 4, 4, 4), work Cable Patt over next 20 sts, p72 (84, 96, 108, 120, 132), work Cable Patt over next 20 sts, work Row 2 Lace Eyelet Patt over next 36 sts, work Cable Patt over next 20 sts, p72 (84, 96, 108, 120, 132), work Cable Patt over next 20 sts, p0 (0, 0, 4, 4, 4).

Next row (RS): K0 (0, 0, 4, 4, 4), work Cable Patt over next 20 sts, k72 (84, 96, 108, 120, 132), work Cable Patt over next 20 sts, work Row 3 Lace Eyelet Patt over next 36 sts, work Cable Patt over next 20 sts, k72 (84, 96, 108, 120, 132), work Cable Patt over next 20 sts, k0 (0, 0, 4, 4, 4).

Next row (WS): P0 (0, 0, 4, 4, 4), work Cable Patt over next 20 sts, p72 (84, 96, 108, 120, 132), work Cable Patt over next 20 sts, work Row 4 Lace Eyelet Patt over next 36 sts, work Cable Patt over next 20 sts, p72 (84, 96, 108, 120, 132), work Cable Patt over next 20 sts, p0 (0, 0, 4, 4, 4).

Continue in established patt until piece measures 14½ (14½, 15, 15½, 16, 16½)"/37 (37, 38, 39, 41, 42)cm from beg, end with a RS row facing for next row.

Divide for Armholes:

See note on binding off.

Next row (RS): Work in patt as established over first 58 (64, 69, 77, 83, 89) sts, BO the next 14 (14, 16, 16, 16, 16) sts for underarm, cont in patt as established over following 116 (128, 138, 154, 166, 178) sts, BO next 14 (14, 16, 16, 16, 16) sts for underarm, work in patt as established to end.

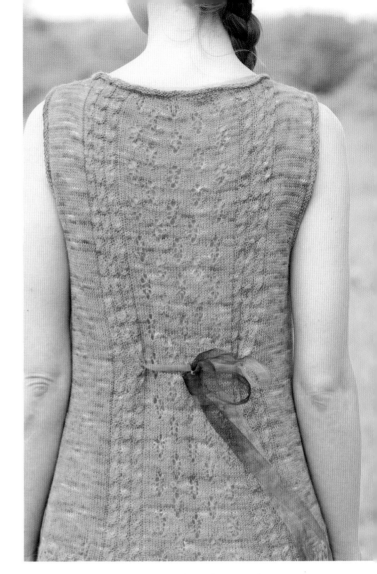

Left Front:

Next row (WS): Work even in patt over first 58 (64, 69, 77, 83, 89) sts, turn (this is armhole edge). Place 116 (128, 138, 154, 166, 178) sts on a stitch holder for Back and the rem 58 (64, 69, 77, 83, 89) sts on a 2nd stitch holder for Right Front.

Shape V-neck:

Next row (RS): K to last 22 sts, k2tog, work Cable Patt over rem 20 sts—57 (63, 68, 76, 82, 88) sts.

Next row (WS): Work Cable Patt over first 20 sts, p2tog, purl to end—56 (62, 67, 75, 81, 87) sts.

Rep last 2 rows 4 (4, 5, 4, 3, 2) more times—48 (54, 57, 67, 75, 83) sts rem.

Next row (RS): K to last 22 sts, k2tog, work Cable Patt over rem 20 sts—47 (53, 56, 66, 74, 82) sts.

Next row (WS): Work even in patt as established.

Rep last 2 rows 26 (28, 27, 30, 33, 36) more times—21 (25, 29, 36, 41, 46) sts rem.

Work even until armhole measures 7 (7½, 7½, 8, 8½, 9)"/18 (19, 19, 20, 22, 23) cm from beg of shaping, end with a WS row.

Shape Shoulder:

See note on binding off.

Next row (RS): BO 7 (8, 10, 12, 14, 15) sts at beg of next row—14 (17, 19, 24, 27, 31) sts.

Next row: Work even in patt.

Rep last 2 rows.

BO rem 7 (9, 9, 12, 13, 16) sts.

Back:

Return to 116 (128, 138, 154, 166, 178) sts on holder for Back, rejoin yarn to left-hand side so that WS row is facing for next row.

Work in established patt until Back measures the same as Left Front to shoulder shaping.

Shape Shoulders:

BO 7 (8, 10, 12, 14, 15) sts at beg of next 4 rows—88 (96, 98, 106, 110, 118) sts.

BO 7 (9, 9, 12, 13, 16) sts on following 2 rows.

BO rem 74 (78, 80, 82, 84, 86) sts.

Right Front:

Return to 58 (64, 69, 77, 83, 89) sts on holder for Right Front, rejoin yarn to left-hand side so that WS row is facing for next row.

Work WS row even in patt.

Next row (RS): Work Cable Patt over first 20 sts, ssk, k to end—57 (63, 68, 76, 82, 88) sts.

Next row (WS): Purl to last 22 sts, p2tog-tbl, work Cable Patt over rem 20 sts—56 (62, 67, 75, 81, 87) sts.

Rep last 2 rows 4 (4, 5, 4, 3, 2) more times—48 (54, 57, 67, 75, 83) sts rem.

Next row (RS): Work Cable Patt over first 20 sts, ssk, k to end—47 (53, 56, 66, 74, 82) sts.

Next row (WS): Work even in patt as established.

Rep last 2 rows 26 (28, 27, 30, 33, 36) more times—21 (25, 29, 36, 41, 46) sts rem.

Work even until armhole measures 7 (7½, 7½, 8, 8½, 9)"/18 (19, 19, 20, 22, 23)cm from beg of shaping, end with a RS row.

Shape Shoulder:

Next row (WS): BO 7 (8, 10, 12, 14, 15) sts at beg of next row—14 (17, 19, 24, 27, 31) sts.

Next row: Work even in patt as established.

Rep last 2 rows.

BO rem 7 (9, 9, 12, 13, 16) sts.

Armhole Edging:

With RS facing, working across armhole edge, pick up and k 130 (138, 138, 146, 156, 164) sts.

Work 2 rows in Seed st.

Beg with a purl row, work 5 rows in St st.

BO using method in notes.

Rep for 2nd armhole.

Front Edging:

With RS facing, beg at lower edge, pick up and k 154 (154, 160, 164, 170, 174) up Right Front edge, 70 (74, 76, 78, 80, 82) sts across back neck, and 154 (154, 160, 164, 170, 174) down Left Front edge—378 (382, 396, 406, 420, 430) sts total.

Work 2 rows in Seed st.

Beg with a p row, work 5 rows in St st.

BO using method in notes.

FINISHING

Cut ribbon into 4 equal lengths. Or make four I-cord each 27"/68cm long.

Mark points on each Cable Patt on Back 11½ (11½, 11¾, 12, 12¼, 12½)"/29 (29, 30, 30, 31, 32) cm from lower edge. With aid of a safety pin, wiggle the ribbon (or I-cord) through from RS to WS of vest and stitch in place.

Mark similar points on each center front edge 11½ (11½, 11¾, 12, 12¼, 12½)"/29 (29, 30, 30, 31, 32)cm from lower edge and sew ribbon (or I-cord) to the inside of rolled edging.

To secure and prevent the back neck stretching, using a (3.25mm) D/3 size crochet hook, work a row of single crochet across the back neck, working into the pick-up row, easing the width of the neck slightly as you go.

Schematic

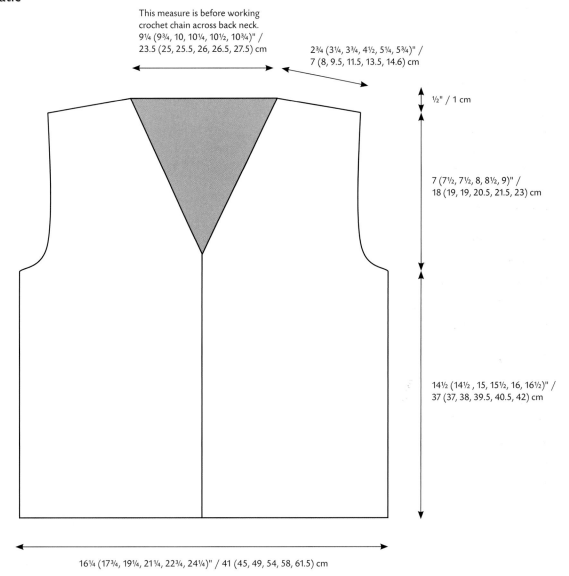

This measure is before working crochet chain across back neck.
9¼ (9¾, 10, 10¼, 10½, 10¾)" /
23.5 (25, 25.5, 26, 26.5, 27.5) cm

2¾ (3¼, 3¾, 4½, 5¼, 5¾)" /
7 (8, 9.5, 11.5, 13.5, 14.6) cm

½" / 1 cm

7 (7½, 7½, 8, 8½, 9)" /
18 (19, 19, 20.5, 21.5, 23) cm

14½ (14½ , 15, 15½, 16, 16½)" /
37 (37, 38, 39.5, 40.5, 42) cm

16¼ (17¾, 19¼, 21¼, 22¾, 24¼)" / 41 (45, 49, 54, 58, 61.5) cm

Chart A

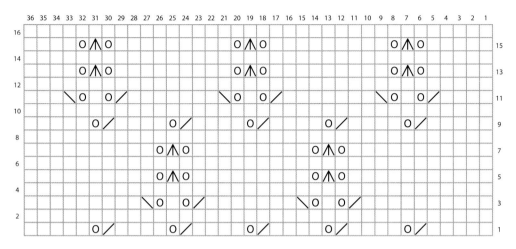

Note: Chart reads right to left for RS rows and left to right for WS rows.

Key

	Knit
	Knit on RS rows, purl on WS rows.

	K2tog
	Knit 2 stitches together (right-slanting decrease).

	SSK
	Slip 2 stitches individually as if to knit, then knit those 2 stitches together through the back of loops (left-slanting decrease).

	YO
O	Yarn over (increases 1 stitch).

	CDD
	Slip 2 stitches as if to k2tog, k1, pass the 2 slipped stitches over.

Caged Beauty Top

DESIGNER: Nicole Feller-Johnson SKILL LEVEL: Intermediate/Advanced

This asymmetrical shell combines double-stranded lace weight Stockinette with a striped and slipped-stitch lace wedge to create a feminine, modern feel. Pair this silky, lofty sweater with a pencil skirt or cigarette pants for day wear, or with jeans or a miniskirt and tights for a fabulous night out!

SIZES
S (M, L, 1X)

FINISHED MEASUREMENTS
Bust 32 (36, 40, 44)"/81 (91, 102, 112)cm

Length 22 (23½, 26, 27½)"/56 (59.5, 66, 70)cm, not including strap

MATERIALS AND TOOLS
Neighborhood Fiber Co. Loft (60% mohair/40% silk; 1oz/29g = 330yd/300m): (A), 3 (4, 4, 5) hanks, color Georgetown; (B), 1 (1, 1, 2) hanks, color Ward Circle—approx 1320 (1650, 1650, 2310)yd/1200 (1500, 1500, 2100)m of lace weight yarn (0)

Neighborhood Fiber Co. Maisonette (50% merino/50% tussah silk; 4oz/113g = 1250yd/1143m): (C), 1 hank, color Del Ray—approx 315 (500, 625, 950) yd/288 (457, 572, 869)m of lace weight yarn (0)

Knitting needles: 3.75mm (size 5 U.S.) 32"/80cm circular needle and one pair of straight needles or size to obtain gauge

Removable and ring stitch markers

Tapestry needle

2 lightweight removable clip stitch markers

2 dpns (for grafting lower point of bodice)

GAUGE
20 sts/32 rows = 4"/10cm with 2 strands of A held together in St st, after blocking

24 sts/32 rows = 4"/10cm in Lace pattern with a single strand of yarn, after blocking

Note: A 4mm (size 6 U.S.) needle might be needed to obtain row gauge.

Always take time to check your gauge.

SPECIAL ABBREVIATIONS
M1L (Make One Left) – With left needle tip, lift strand between needles from front to back. Knit the lifted strand through the back.

M1R (Make One Right) – With left needle tip, lift strand between needles from back to front. Knit the lifted strand through the front.

INSTRUCTIONS

Bodice:

Beg at top edge of Bodice, with circular needle and 2 strands of A held tog, CO 140 (160, 180, 200) sts. Join in the rnd, being careful not to twist.

Purl 1 rnd.

Next rnd: P35 (40, 45, 50), place removable marker on st below (this stays in place as you work rest of piece, and does not slip with each row), p35 (40, 45, 50), place ring marker on needle, p35 (40, 45, 50), place removable marker on st below, p35 (40, 45, 50), place ring marker for end of rnd. Note: The removable markers indicate strap placement after Bodice is fully worked.

Knit 1 rnd.

Purl 1 rnd.

Knit 1 rnd.

Section 1 (Increase):

Rnd 1: K2, M1L, k to 2 sts before first ring marker (hereafter ring markers are referred to simply as "marker"), M1R, k2, sl marker, k2, M1L, k to 2 sts before end marker, M1R, k2—144 (164, 184, 204) sts.

Rnds 2–4: Knit.

Rep these 4 rnds 4 (4, 5, 5) more times for a total of 20 (20, 24, 24) rnds in this section—160 (180, 204, 224) sts.

Section 2 (Increase):

Note: "Center marker" is first ring marker (not beg of rnd marker).

Rnd 1: K to 2 sts before center marker, M1R, k2, sl marker, k2, M1L, k to end of rnd—162 (182, 206, 226) sts.

Rnds 2–8: Knit.

Rep these 8 rnds once more—164 (184, 208, 228) sts.

Rep Rnds 1–6—166 (186, 210, 230) sts.

Begin Opening for Lace Insert:

Rnd 7: Knit to end of rnd, TURN.

Row 8 (WS): Purl, TURN. You have divided your work and will no longer be working in the round. Work back and forth in rows on circular needle as if working with straight needles. RS of fabric should now be facing.

Section 3 (Lace Insert Opening):

Row 1 (RS): K1, p1, k1, ssk, k1, ssk, k to 2 sts before center marker, M1R, k2, sl marker, k2, M1L, k to last 8 sts, k2tog, k1, k2tog, k1, p1, k1—164 (184, 208, 228) sts.

Row 2 (WS): P1, k1, p1, p2tog-tbl, p to last 5 sts, p2tog, p1, k1, p1—162 (182, 206, 226) sts.

Row 3: K1, p1, k1, ssk, k to last 5 sts, k2tog, k1, p1, k1—160 (180, 204, 224) sts.

Rows 4–7: Rep last 2 rows twice—152 (172, 196, 216) sts.

Row 8: Rep Row 2—150 (170, 194, 214) sts.

Rep these 8 rows until you have 10 sts on each side of the center marker, 20 sts total, ending with a WS row. Remove markers.

Next row (RS): K1, p1, k1, ssk, k to last 5, k2tog, k1, p1, k1—18 sts.

Next row: P1, k1, p1, p2tog-tbl, p to last 5 sts, p2tog, p1, k1, p1—16 sts.

Rep last 2 rows until 6 sts rem.

With RS facing place first 3 sts on a dpn, place last 3 sts on another dpn, hold dpns with WS of sts tog and graft the sts tog using Kitchener stitch, or you may sew if desired. Break yarn and weave in ends. Lightly spray block.

Lace Insert:

With circular needle and 2 strands of C held tog, using a long-tail cast-on, CO 178 (190, 214, 226) sts. Work back and forth in rows as if working with straight needles.

Purl 4 rows.

Knit 1 row.

Break one strand of C and prepare to work chart with the single rem strand.

Chart:

Work chart rows 1–19. On RS, work from right to left, repeating between sts 21 and 26 as needed for your size and shown on chart between red lines. On WS, work from left to right, completing all sts AS THEY ARE REPRESENTED. There is no need for you to change from K to P, etc., on the WS.

Add another strand of C and hold the 2 strands tog. Continue working chart until chart is complete and only 1 st rem. Fasten off.

Helpful hint: To avoid tangles, break A and C after every 2 consecutive rows of where they are worked, carry B loosely up sides of piece. As a result, you will have all the ends of A on one side of the triangle, and all the ends of C on the other side of the triangle.

Gently weave all ends into selvedge. Block to gauge.

Sew Lace Insert into Bodice: With RS facing, pin Lace Insert into side opening of Bodice beginning at the top point of the Insert and working down. Ease in gently, leaving some of the Bodice triangle to hang lower than Insert if a more modern look is desired. Sew Insert in place using mattress stitch.

Front Strap:

Note: This assumes it will be worn on your left shoulder.

With straight needles and 2 strands of A held tog, CO 44 sts.

Knit 1 row. Break one strand and continue with single strand only.

Purl 1 row.

Chart:

Note: While working chart, at the beginning and end of every row, create selvedge by working k1, p1, k1 edges on RS and p1, k1, p1 edges on WS.

Work chart between sts 21 and 46, repeating between sts 21 and 26 four times, until your strap contains (horizontally) 3 cage motif repeats. Continue in straight pattern with no further decreases 5 times or until strap is desired length.

With C, knit 1 row.

BO.

Back Strap:

Work same as Front Strap but work chart columns 1–26, causing the decreases to be on the opposite side of the strap. BO.

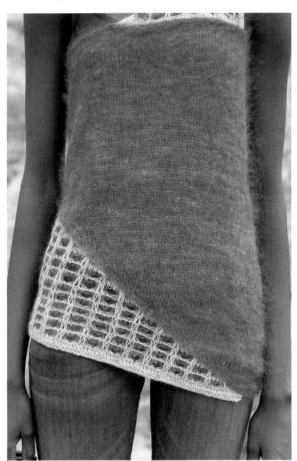

Block straps. With RS facing, sew BO edges of straps tog. Weave in all ends.

FINISHING

Sew strap to bodice: Find center front removable stitch marker. When you are looking at your bodice the lace wedge should face your left side, and you will be sewing the strap to what faces your right hand side. This will make the piece as you wear it have a left shoulder strap and a right hip lace inset.

With RS facing, place Front Strap CO edge 2"/5cm across center removable marker and sew in place.

Turn piece over and find back center removable marker. With RS facing, place Back Strap CO edge 2"/5cm across center removable marker and sew in place. You should now have a bodice with a gently curving left shoulder strap sewn in place and no WS areas of your work should show anywhere.

At what is now your armscye (the straight selvedge of the lace strap), with 2 strands of C held tog, pick up 3 sts from bodice. Use these to make a 3-st applied I-cord edging up and back down the straight selvedge of your strap. Sew remaining 3 I-cord sts to 3 sts on opposite side of bodice, and weave in ends.

Wear with confidence and enjoy!

Schematic

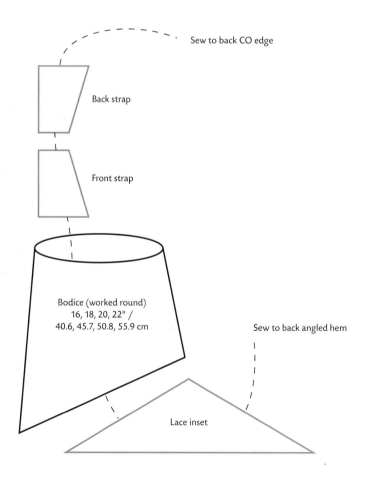

Sew to back CO edge

Back strap

Front strap

Bodice (worked round)
16, 18, 20, 22" /
40.6, 45.7, 50.8, 55.9 cm

Sew to back angled hem

Lace inset

Chart A

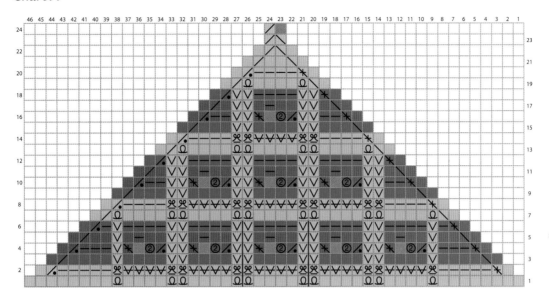

Key

Knit
Knit

Knit-tbl
K1-tbl on RS. P1-tbl on WS.

K2tog
Knit 2 stitches together as 1 stitch.

Purl
Purl on RS. Knit on WS.

P1 Elongated Twice
Purl and yarn over twice. Yarn overs to be dropped on following row.

P2tog
Purl 2 together on RS. Knit 2 together on WS.

Sl
Slip

Sl wyib
Slip with yarn in back on RS. Slip as if to purl with yarn in front on WS.

SPP
Slip purl psso on RS. Slip 1 k1, psso on WS.

SSK
Slip 1 stitch as if to knit. Slip another stitch as if to knit. Insert LH needle into front of these 2 stitches and knit them together on RS. On WS slip 1 stitch as if to purl. Slip another stitch as if to purl. Purl slipped stitches together.

No Stitch
Placeholder—No stitch made.

Yo2x
Yarn over twice.

Plied Stripes Sweater

DESIGNER: Michelle Hunter SKILL LEVEL: Easy

Magically turn lace weight yarn into worsted weight yarn with Navajo knitting, also known as chain plying. Navajo knitting triple plies yarn from one skein without cutting or dividing the skein. The triple-stranded yarn is then worked on a needle size appropriate for worsted weight yarn for quick knitting.

This sweater features opaque and sheer stripes created by alternating triple- and single-stranded yarn sourced from one skein. The casual, oversized style is easy to wear and knit.

SIZES
S (M, L, 1X)

FINISHED MEASUREMENTS
Bust 37 (41, 46, 50)"/94 (104, 117, 127)cm

Length 20¼ (21¼, 22¼, 23½)"/51 (54, 57, 59)cm

MATERIALS AND TOOLS
Schoppel-Wolle Lace Ball (75% virgin wool/25% nylon; 3.5oz/100g = 875yd/800m): 2 (3, 3, 3) balls #1963— approx 1700 (2000, 2300, 2600)yd/1554 (1829, 2103, 2377)m of lace weight yarn 🧶

Knitting needles: 4.5mm (size 7 U.S.) or size to obtain gauge

4mm (size 6 U.S.) 16"/40cm circular (for neckband and sleeve cuffs only)

Stitch holder

Spare needle (for 3-needle bind-off)

Yarn needle

GAUGE
22 sts/32 rows = 4"/10cm using larger needles with triple-plied yarn in St st

Always take time to check your gauge.

SPECIAL ABBREVIATIONS
M1L (Make One Left) – With left needle tip, lift strand between needles from front to back. Knit the lifted strand through the back.

M1R (Make One Right) – With left needle tip, lift strand between needles from back to front. Knit the lifted strand through the front.

PATTERN STITCH

Plied Stripes Pattern (18 row repeat):

Rows 1–4: Beginning with a (RS) row and single-ply yarn, work 4 rows in St st.

Rows 5 and 6: With triple-plied yarn, knit 2 rows (one Garter ridge).

Rows 7–10: With single-ply yarn, work 4 rows in St st.

Rows 11–18: With triple-plied yarn, work 8 rows in St st.

INSTRUCTIONS

Note:

For a tutorial on Navajo knitting, see knitpurlhunter.com/blog/?p=1320.

Back and Front (make 2)

Hem:

With larger needle and triple-plied yarn, CO 96 (108, 120, 132) sts.

Work in Garter St (knit every row) for 8 rows.

Inc row (RS): K4, M1R, k to last 4 sts, M1L, k4—98 (110, 122, 134) sts.

Next row (WS): K4, p to last 4 sts, k4.

Rep last 2 rows twice—102 (114, 126, 138)sts.

Work evenly for 4 rows.

Body:

Work Plied Stripes Patt until piece measures 12 (12½, 13, 13½)"/31 (32, 33, 34)cm from cast-on edge, end with a WS row.

Sleeves:

Next row (RS): CO 6 sts, cont in Plied Stripes Patt to end of row—108 (120, 132, 144) sts.

Rep last row 7 more times—150 (162, 174, 186) sts.

Work even until piece measures approx 19½ (20½, 21½, 22½)"/50 (52, 55, 57)cm from cast-on edge, ending after Row 12 (WS) of Plied Stripes Patt.

Neck Shaping:

Next row (RS): Cont with triple-plied yarn, k 54 (59, 64, 70) sts, place rem sts on holder. Work each side of neck separately in triple-plied St st.

Next row (WS): Purl to end of row.

Next (RS) and following 3 rows (dec): Dec 1 st at neck edge.

Place these 50 (55, 60, 66) sts on holder.

With RS facing, return sts from holder to needles and rejoin yarn. BO center 42 (44, 46, 46) sts. Complete to match first side, reversing shaping.

Place remaining 50 (55, 60, 66) sts on holder.

FINISHING

Block to schematic measurements.

Using 3-needle BO technique, join shoulder seams tog.

Neckband:

Neckband is worked in the round with triple-plied yarn on smaller size circular needles.

With RS facing and beg at left shoulder seam, pick up and knit 2 sts for every 3 rows and 1 st for every BO st.

Adjusting st count to a multiple of 10 on first round if necessary, work in Garter St for 4 rnds.

Dec rnd (WS): *P8, p2tog; repeat from * to end of rnd.

BO.

Sleeve Cuffs:

Cuffs are worked with triple-plied yarn on smaller size circular needles. Work back and forth in rows as if working with straight needles.

With RS facing, pick up and knit 2 sts for every 3 rows along sleeve end.

Adjusting st count to a multiple of 10 on first row if necessary, work in Garter St for 4 rows.

Dec row (WS): *K8, k2tog; repeat from * to end of row.

BO.

Sew side and sleeve seams, leaving lower 2"/5cm of side seam open. Weave in ends.

Schematic

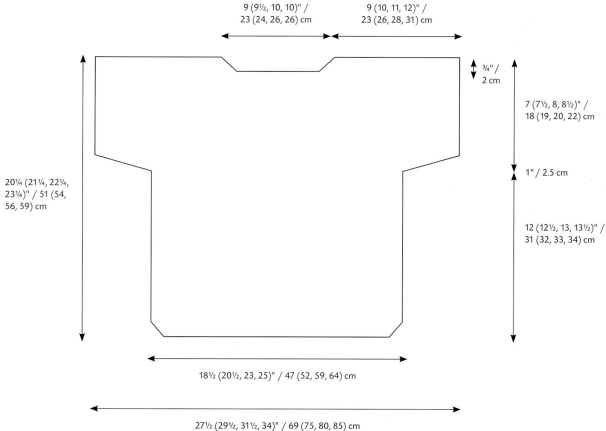

9 (9½, 10, 10)" / 23 (24, 26, 26) cm

9 (10, 11, 12)" / 23 (26, 28, 31) cm

¾" / 2 cm

7 (7½, 8, 8½)" / 18 (19, 20, 22) cm

1" / 2.5 cm

20¼ (21¼, 22¼, 23¼)" / 51 (54, 56, 59) cm

12 (12½, 13, 13½)" / 31 (32, 33, 34) cm

18½ (20½, 23, 25)" / 47 (52, 59, 64) cm

27½ (29½, 31½, 34)" / 69 (75, 80, 85) cm

Farfalle Shawl

DESIGNER: Patty Lyons SKILL LEVEL: Intermediate

This is the perfect layering piece for chilly fall days or cool spring nights. By mixing the moldable crispness of wool stainless steel with the drapey softness of silk mohair, you get a fabric that is fluffy and soft with a stitch pattern that stays crisp and holds its shape.

FINISHED MEASUREMENTS

Width (across top edge) 50"/127cm

Depth (center back) 21"/53cm

MATERIALS AND TOOLS

Lion Brand Yarn LB Collection Silk Mohair (70% super kid mohair/30% silk; 0.88oz/25g = 231yd/212m): (A), 2 skeins, color Sunset #133—approx 461yd/424m of sock weight yarn (1)

Lion Brand Yarn LB Collection Wool Stainless Steel (75% wool/25% stainless steel; 0.50oz/14g = 273yd/244m): (B), 4 cones, color Amber #186—approx 1,092yd/976m of lace weight yarn (0)

Knitting needles: 5mm (size 8 U.S.) 36"/80cm circular needle or size to obtain gauge

Stitch marker

Tapestry needle

GAUGE

22 sts/34 rows = 4"/10cm in Farfalle Stitch, holding 3 strands together (2 strands of B and 1 strand of A)

Always take time to check your gauge.

SPECIAL ABBREVIATIONS

M1L (Make One Left) – With left needle tip, lift strand between needles from front to back. Knit the lifted strand through the back.

M1R (Make One Right) – With left needle tip, lift strand between needles from back to front. Knit the lifted strand through the front.

LS3 (Lifted Stitch Three) – Insert RH needle under 3 floats and knit next stitch, pulling the new stitch down and catching floats on RS row. Insert RH needle under the 3 floats and lift them up onto the LH needle; purl lifts together with middle stitch on WS row.

PATTERN STITCH

Farfalle Stitch (for gauge, swatch multiple of 6 sts + 3):

Rows 1, 3, and 5 (RS): K1, *k1, sl 5 wyif; rep from * to last 2 sts, k2.

Rows 2 and 4 (WS): Purl.

Row 6: P2, *p2, LS3, p3; rep from * to last st, p1.

Row 7: Knit.

Rows 8, 10, and 12: P1, sl 1 wyib, *sl 2 wyib, p1, sl 3 wyib; rep from * to last st, p1.

When working the increases on the chart, work M1R for the first two increases (following Garter St edge and before the center stitch) and the M1L for the second two increases (following the center stitch and before the Garter St edge).

Hold 3 strands tog throughout (2 strands of B and 1 strand of A).

Using long-tail cast on, CO 3 sts.

Row 1 (RS): K1, k2tog—2 sts.

Work 21 rows of Garter Stitch (k every row).

Next row (RS): K2, PM, turn 90 degrees and pick up 11 sts (one for each Garter ridge) across side, PM, pick up 2 sts from cast-on edge—15 sts.

Next row (WS): K2 (this is your Garter edge), sl marker, p5, PM, p1 (this is the center st), PM, p5, sl marker, k2 (this is your Garter edge).

Begin working chart, working first two stitches in Garter st (not shown on chart), work chart using M1R for M, work center stitch (not shown on chart), repeat chart using M1L for M, work last two stitches in Garter st (not shown on chart).

After Row 160 of the chart, work the last row as follows, keeping first and last two stitches in Garter st, and knitting the center stitch:

Half of shawl, work twice: K1, M1R, k1, M1L, k5, *M1R, k1, M1L, k5; rep from * to the last 8 sts, M1R, k1, M1L, k5, M1R, k1, M1L, k1.

FINISHING

BO loosely. To block, pin edges into place, smoothing out the top edge so that it runs straight across. Pin out the scallops on the bind-off edge, mist with water. Let dry.

Rows 9 and 11: Knit.

Row 13: K1, *LS3, k5; rep from * to last 2 sts, LS3, k1.

Row 14: Purl.

INSTRUCTIONS

Notes:

The shawl starts at the center back of the neck and is knit down to the bottom edge. To conserve space, only the increase edge stitches (in the black box) and the center repeat (in the red box) are shown in the chart.

The chart is shown for one half of the shawl. You will need to repeat it again after the center st (which is not shown on the chart). Knit the first and last 2 sts on every row (these sts are not shown on the chart).

Chart continued on opposite page

**Repeat rows
22-76 for rows
106-160**

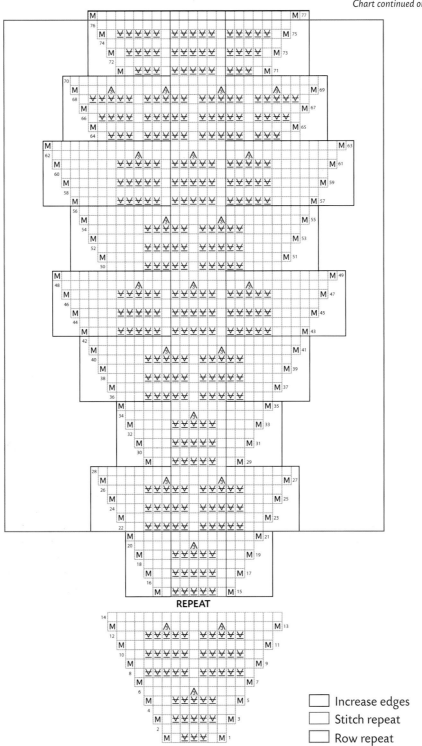

REPEAT

	Increase edges
	Stitch repeat
	Row repeat

Chart continued from opposite page

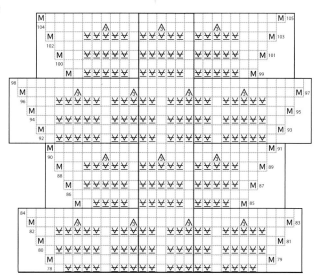

Key

Stockinette
Knit on right side, purl on wrong side.

M1R (for the right side of the shawl)
Make 1 Right: Insert the LH needle, from back to front, under the strand of yarn between the needles. Knit lifted loop through the front.

M1L (for the left side of the shawl)
Make One Left: insert the LH needle, from front to back, under the strand of yarn between the needles. Knit lifted loop through the back.

Sl1wyif
Slip stitch purlwise with yarn in front on RS rows.

Sl1wyib
Slip stitch purlwise with yarn in back on WS rows.

Lifted Stitch Three
Insert RH needle under 3 floats and knit next stitch, pulling the new stitch down and catching floats on the RS rows; Insert the RH needle under the 3 floats and lift them up onto the LH needle, purl lifts together with middle stitch on WS rows.

about the author

Carol J. Sulcoski is a former attorney turned knitting designer, author, hand dyer and teacher. She is author of *Sock Yarn Studio* (Lark Crafts 2012); *Knitting Socks With Handpainted Yarns* (Interweave Press 2009) and co-author of *Knit So Fine: Knitting With Skinny Yarns* (Interweave Press 2008). Her designs have been published in *Vogue Knitting*, *Interweave Knits, Creative Knitting Magazine, Noro Magazine*, and other books and magazines. Her technical articles also frequently appear in premier knitting magazines like *Vogue Knitting*. She is the founder of Black Bunny Fibers (www.blackbunnyfibers.com), a boutique handdyeing business selling unique yarns, fibers and patterns. She lives outside Philadelphia with her family.

about the contributors

Véronik Avery is a member of the Brooklyn Tweed Design Team, and author of *Knitting 24/7* (Stewart, Tabori & Chang 2010) and *Knitting Classic Style* (STC 2007). Her work has appeared in more than 30 books and publications such as *Weekend Knitting* (STC 2009), *Handknit Holidays* (STC 2005), *Reversible Knitting* (STC 2009), *Vogue Knitting, Interweave Knits* and others. She lives outside Montreal with her family.

Marlaina "Marly" Bird fled the world of financial services to launch her Yarn Thing podcast and hasn't looked back since. She's the co-author of *Curvy Crochet* (Leisure Arts 2011), *I Can't Believe I'm Knitting Entrelac* (Leisure Arts 2014), and *Knitting for Dummies* 3rd ed. (Wiley 2013), and creative director for Bijou Basin Ranch Yarns. Marly's designs have appeared in many knitting and crochet magazines, including *Love of Crochet, Knitter's Magazine, Knit Simple, Interweave Crochet, Knitscene*, and *Inside Crochet*, and in many knitting and crochet books. In her spare time she raises three kids with her husband in suburban Denver. Her website is www.marlybird.com.

Barbara J. Brown is a designer and lifelong knitter who lives in Alberta, Canada. She is the author of *Knitting Kneehighs: Sock Styles from Classic to Contemporary* (Krause Publications 2011). Her designs have appeared in *Vogue Knitting, Yarn Forward, The Knitter* (UK) and other publications and she has designed for yarn companies such as Koigu and Ancient Arts Fibre Crafts. Barb also teaches at various community colleges, fibre events, retreats, and yarn shops.

Fiona Ellis graduated with a Bachelor of Arts in Fashion Knitwear Design from DeMontfort University, England in 1993, and is the author of *Inspired Cable Knits, Inspired Fair Isle Knits*, and *Knitspiration Journal* (all from Potter Craft). Her work is regularly featured in fine knitting magazines including *Vogue Knitting, Twist Collective, Creative Knitting*, and *Knitter's Magazine*. Her website is fionaellisonline.com.

Nicole Feller-Johnson is a Philadelphia-based knitwear designer and author with a BFA from the University of the Arts. She is the owner of No Two Snowflakes, an online yarn and pattern shop featuring several designers, as well as her own design line, Nicole Feller-Johnson, comprised of bespoke pieces and fine art work, seen at nicolefeller-johnson.squarespace.com.

Erika Flory has been designing knitwear for babies and toddlers for more than 20 years, and offers patterns and kits on her website, www.kidknits.biz. Her designs have appeared in the knitting webzines *KnitNet, For the Love of Yarn, Knotions, The Daily Knitter*, and *Petite Purls*, as well as in the WEBS online and print catalogs for Valley Yarns, and for Pisgah Yarn & Dyeing. Her book of patterns, *Head to Toe Knits: 23 Designs to Knit for Baby*, is available through lulu.com. Not a day goes by that she doesn't touch yarn.

Franklin Habit is a Chicago-based designer of handknits and the author of *It Itches: A Stash of Knitting Cartoons* (Interweave Press 2008). He contributes regularly to major fiber arts publications and is the proprietor of the popular knitting blog *The Panopticon* (www.the-panopticon.blogspot.com).

Michelle Hunter is best known as the creator of the knitting education website, *Knit Purl Hunter*. She divides her time between teaching classes nationwide and online instruction. Her books, *Building Blocks* and *Building in Color*, are skill-building series designed to progress the knitter through the major knitting principles. Her designs have been featured in various publications and are all supported with video tutorials. She considers herself the luckiest person alive to be able to combine her passion for teaching with her love of knitting.

Patty Lyons (www.pattylyons.com) is a knitting teacher and designer who teaches nationally at guilds and shows around the country such as *Vogue Knitting LIVE*, *Knit and Crochet Show*, and *Stitches*. Her classes can also be found online at *Craftsy* and *Knitting Daily*. After running a yarn store in NYC, in 2008 Patty joined Lion Brand Yarn, where she served as the Studio Director and head of the education department for five years. Patty's designs and knitting articles can be found in *Vogue Knitting*, *Creative Knitting*, *Knit 1, 2, 3,* and *Knit 'N Style* magazine.

Elizabeth Morrison lives with her husband and two sons in Madison, Wisconsin. She learned to knit as a child, but it didn't really take until the late 1980s. See more of her work at www.sweaterstudio.com or find her on Ravelry as ElizabethSABLE.

Brooke Nico began her designing activities by sewing her own wardrobe, inspired by drape and color. She brought her talents to knitting almost 10 years ago, first exploring modular construct, then lace. In 2006, Brooke opened Kirkwood Knittery, a local yarn shop located in St. Louis, MO. As a dedicated teacher, Brooke guides knitters through the intricacies of techniques to make their projects as polished as possible. Her first book, *Lovely Knitted Lace*, was published by Lark Crafts in spring 2014.

Robyn Schrager began knitting as a child to avoid the ignomy of being sick on a roller coaster, and never regretted the choice. As co-owner of Kirkwood Knittery her designs are often developed with the purpose of showcasing yarns in unexpected ways, and and are approachable by knitters at all skill levels. She loves stripes (despite not really having the silhouette to pull them off herself). Her designs have been featured in *Creative Knitting* and *Knit Simple* and she has designed for yarn companies such as Koigu, Skacel and Tahki/Stacy Charles.

Andi Smith is the author of *Big Foot Knits* (Cooperative Press 2013). She is a teacher, autism advocate, and passionate knitter and crocheter. Originally hailing from Yorkshire, England, Andi now lives in the USA. You can find her on ravelry/fb/twitter under the name knitbrit, and read about her adventures at www.blog.knitbrit.com.

knitting abbreviations

ABBR.	DESCRIPTION	ABBR.	DESCRIPTION	ABBR.	DESCRIPTION	ABBR.	DESCRIPTION
[ ]	work instructions within brackets as many times as directed	dec	decrease/ decreases/ decreasing	M1L	make 1 st slanting to left; 1st increased	skp	slip, knit, pass stitch over; 1 st decreased
( )	work instructions within parentheses as many times as directed	dpn	double pointed needle(s)	oz	ounce(s)	sk2p	slip 1, knit 2 together, pass slip stitch over the knit 2 together; 2 st decreased
**	repeat instructions following the asterisks as directed	foll	follow/follows/ following	p or P	purl	sl	slip
*	repeat instructions following the single asterisk as directed	g	gram	pat(s) or patt	patterns	sl st	slip stitch(es)
"	inch	inc	increase/ increases/ increasing	PM	place marker	ssk	slip, slip, knit these 2 stitches together; 1 st decrease
alt	alternate	k or K	knit	prev	previous	st(s)	stitch(es)
approx	approximately	kfb	knit through front and back loops of stitch; 1 st increased	psso	pass slipped stitch over	St st	stockinette stitch/stocking stitch
beg	begin/beginning	k2tog	knit 2 stitches together	p2sso	pass 2 slipped stiches over	tbl	through back loop
bet	between	K3tog	knit 3 stitches together	p2tog	purl 2 stitches together	tog	together
BO	bind off	LH	left hand	rem	remain/ remaining	WS	wrong side
CC	contrasting color	m	meter(s)	rep	repeat(s)	wyib	with yarn in back
cm	centimeter(s)	MC	main color	rev St st	reverse stockinette stitch	wyif	with yarn in front
cn	cable needle	mm	millimeter(s)	RH	right hand	yd(s)	yard(s)
CO	cast on	M1	make 1 stitch	rnd(s)	round(s)	yo	yarn over
cont	continue	M1R	make 1 st slanting to right; 1 st increased	RS	right side		

yarn sources

Ancient Arts Fibre Crafts
(BFL Lace, 75% Merino/25% Silk Lace)
www.ancientartsfibre.com

Bijou Basin Ranch (Seraphim)
www.bijoubasinranch.com

Black Bunny Fibers (Heavenly Lace,
Merino-Silk Lace, Suri Sparkle Lace)
www.blackbunnyfibers.com

Buffalo Wool (Heaven)
The Buffalo Wool Co.
604 Joy Ln.
Kennedale, TX 76060
www.thebuffalowoolco.com

Cephalopod Yarns (Nautilace)
www.cephalopodyarns.com

Classic Elite Yarns (Pirouette)
16 Esquire Rd, Unit 2
North Billerica, MA
1-800-343-0308
www.classiceliteyarns.com

Fiesta Yarns (Gracie's Lace)
5620 Venice Ave. NE, Suite J
Albuquerque, NM 87113
www.fiestayarns.com

Habu Textiles (Cotton Nerimaki Slub)
99 Madison Ave.
Suite 503
New York, NY 10016
www.habutextiles.com

Koigu Wool Co. (KPPM, Koigu Bulky)
Chatsworth , Ontario
Canada N0H 1G0
1-888-765-WOOL
www.koigu.com

Lion Brand (LB Collection Stainless Steel;
LB Collection Silk Mohair)
135 Kero Rd.
Carlstadt, NJ 07072
800-661-7551
www.lionbrand.com

Lorna's Laces (Helen's Lace)
4229 N. Honore St.
Chicago, IL 60613
773-935-3803
www.lornaslaces.net

Lotus Yarns (Mimi)
Trendsetter Yarns
16745 Saticoy St. #101
Van Nuys CA 91406
www.trendsetter.com/lotusyarns

Malabrigo (Silky Alpaca Lace)
786-866-6187
www.malabrigoyarn.com

Neighborhood Fiber Co. (Loft, Maisonette)
www.neighborhoodfiberco.com

S. Charles Collezione (Celine)
Tahki Stacy Charles, Inc.
70-60 83rd St Building 12
Glendale, NY 11385
http://tahkistacycharles.com/

Skacel (Schoppel Lace Ball, Schulana Kid-Seta)
Skacel Collection, Inc.
800-255-1278
www.skacelknitting.com

Three Fates Yarns (Lacheis)
http://www.etsy.com/shop/ThreeFatesKnitting

Triskelion Yarn and Fibre (Gofannnon 4-ply)
http://www.triskelion-yarn.com/

Valley Yarns (Colrain Lace)
WEBS: America's Yarn Store
75 Service Center Rd
Northampton, MA 01060
800-FOR-WEBS
www.yarn.com

Westminster Fibers (Regia Silk, Rowan Fine Lace,
Rowan Kidsilk Haze)
8 Shelter Drive
Greer, SC 29650
www.knitrowan.com

dedication

For my beloved brother Mike, whose extensive experience with
fishing line makes him a fine yarn expert himself.

acknowledgments

As always, great thanks to my agent Linda Roghaar, for taking such good care of me, and to the folks at Lark Crafts and Sterling Publishing for their enthusiasm and support. It is not always true that too many cooks spoil the soup: this book was made infinitely better by outstanding editors Amanda Carestio, Shannon Quinn-Tucker, Jennifer Williams, Connie Santisteban, and Deborah Stack, who were a pleasure to work with.

This book gave me the chance to collaborate with some of my favorite people in the knitting industry: the designers who contributed their beautiful projects to this book. Some are longtime friends and others are new friends, but they were all wonderful to work with. I appreciate their patience, good humor and terrific designs.

Special thanks to photographer and stylist Carrie Bostick Hoge. Her photographs reveal the beauty of each project with elegance and style, and her charming personality made the process fun. Thanks to Cecily Glowik McDonald for spending her birthday on a photo shoot with us; to the absolutely gorgeous models Carrie found: Ashley, Chloe, Nyanen, Senetra, and of course my own Grace, and to the Portland, Maine boutique Bliss for providing clothing and accessories for the photo shoots.

Thanks to my technical editor, KJ Hay, for her painstaking work in keeping the math right, and to Amy Trombat for finessing the book's lovely design.

Knitting many projects on a short deadline often requires the use of test knitters; much thanks to Elizabeth Durand, Erika Flory, Mindy Wilson, and Heather Vance. Laura Singewald has my undying gratitude for finishing the pillow cover so beautifully (and quickly!). Thanks as well to the yarn companies who provided so many gorgeous yarns to work with. Thank you to Fiona Ellis and Brooke Nico, for allowing me to quote their wisdom in the first chapter.

A special thanks to my dear knitting and online friends. I have been fortunate to have been befriended by an amazing group of talented, warm-hearted, funny people, far too many to name individually– but I would be remiss in not mentioning dear friends Barb, Brooke, Elizabeth, Laura, Kristi, and Véronik, who serve on the front lines when it comes to the daily battle of keeping me sane, and Trisha, mentor/friend extraordinaire.

And of course I saved the best for last: my beloved family. James, the newest knitter in the family and purveyor of most excellent chocolate chip cookies; Nick, who is always full of encouragement and is my own personal laugh track; and Grace, spokesmodel, movie buddy, and the one who keeps me humble as well as Boris, who sat by my side as I knit many of these projects, and Charcoal, king among bunnies. And as always, my husband Tom, whose love, humor, and support mean more than I can say.

bibliography

Sock Yarn Studio, Carol J. Sulcoski (Lark Crafts 2012) (technical guidance and patterns using sock yarn).

Knit So Fine, Carol J. Sulcoski, Laura Grutzeck, & Lisa R. Myers (Interweave 2008) (patterns and technical advice for knitting with fine-gauge yarns).

Crochet So Fine, Kristin Omdahl (Interweave 2013) (crochet patterns knit in fine-gauge yarns).

Lovely Knitted Lace, Brooke Nico (Lark Crafts 2013) (exploring lace patterns based on geometric shapes).

index